# I Know Who I Am

A survivor's guide to emotional abuse and reclaiming your voice, your worth, and your life.

**PAMELA D. WHITE**

I Know Who I Am
*A Survivor's Guide to Reclaiming Your Voice, Your Worth, and Your Life*
© 2025 Pamela D. White
All rights reserved.

No part of this publication may be reproduced, stored in a retrieval system, or transmitted in any form or by any means—electronic, mechanical, photocopying, recording, or otherwise—without the prior written permission of the copyright owner, except for brief quotations used in reviews or scholarly works.

This book is for informational and inspirational purposes only. It is not intended to replace professional therapy, counseling, or legal advice. The author is not a licensed mental health professional.

For permissions, inquiries, or to contact the author, please visit: Bloomingdesert.life or pamela.bloomingdesert@gmail.com

ISBN: 978-1-7362017-4-9
Printed in the United States of America

Cover design and interior formatting by independent Fiverr professionals.

First Edition
2025

**PDW PUBLICATIONS**

# Dedication

**I dedicate this book to you.**

The one who made yourself small to keep the peace.
The one who wore the mask, held it all together, and called it love.
The one who doubted your instincts—but kept surviving anyway.

This is for the version of you who stayed quiet for too long.
The one who thought they were the problem.
The one who finally stopped apologizing for being real.

You are not broken.
You are not alone.
And you were never too much.

This book is for your voice.
Your truth.
And your return to yourself.

# Contents

| | |
|---|---|
| Introduction | vii |
| **Part I: The Slow Disappearance** | **1** |
| 1. Red Flags and Rose-Colored Glasses | 5 |
| 2. When You've Been Taught Not to Trust Yourself | 15 |
| 3. Please Hold While I Disappear | 25 |
| 4. Shrinking Was How I Survived | 35 |
| *Interlude: The Good That Kept Me* | 47 |
| 5. Disappearing Into the Background | 51 |
| 6. The Lies I Told Myself to Keep Loving Them | 59 |
| **Part II: The Truth Starts Speaking** | **67** |
| 7. Rules Keep Changing | 69 |
| 8. Why Boundaries Felt Like Betrayal | 83 |
| 9. Healing in the Eye of the Storm | 95 |
| 10. The Thing That Kept Me Alive Was Killing Me | 105 |
| 11. The Moment I Couldn't Pretend Anymore | 117 |
| 12. The Truth Hurts. But So Did the Lie. | 127 |
| 13. The Grief That Doesn't Make Sense | 137 |
| *Interlude: The First Time I Told the Truth* | 147 |
| **Part III: The Return to Myself** | **153** |
| 14. Speaking the Truth Broke Its Power | 155 |
| 15. Realizing It Wasn't My Fault | 165 |
| 16. I Didn't Need to Be Perfect to Be Forgiven | 175 |
| *Interlude: The Masks I Wore* | 185 |

17. When I Finally Stopped Hiding                                      189
18. Self-Love Felt Too Far—So I Started with Self-Respect              199
19. Learning to Trust Myself Again                                     209
20. I Was Protecting Myself from Hurt —And from Help                   219
21. When Being Needed Became My Identity                               229
22. Reclaiming My Power                                                239
   *Interlude: The First Time I Felt Free*                             249
23. Messy, Beautiful, Mine: What Healing Looked Like                   253
24. Truth Changes Everything                                           267

## Part IV: Living Free, Living True                                   277

25. Staying Isn't Always a Failure. Leaving Isn't Always a Cure        279
26. Triggers, Flashbacks, and Emotional Landmines                      291
   *Interlude: What Real Love Looks Like*                              303
27. I Know Who I Am                                                    309
   *Stepping Into Your New Tomorrow*                                   323
   *A Note from Me to You*                                             327

## Acknowledgments                                                     331

## Glossary of Terms                                                   337

# Introduction

Anita Alvarez was competing in the world swimming championships in Budapest. As she was in the water—performing, pushing, striving—she started to sink.

The crowd looked on, expecting her next move. They watched as Anita drifted deeper beneath the surface. Everyone was quietly waiting for her next move as she slowly sank lower and lower. They thought it was part of the performance.

Nobody realized she was unresponsive.

Nobody noticed she was drowning.

Nobody—except her coach.

Coach Andrea Fuentes dove in fully clothed, cutting through the water, and pulled Anita's body to the surface. She saved her life.

Today, I want to be your coach.

Because I see you sinking.

I see you trying to perform, to endure, to survive—while slowly going under. I see your unresponsiveness. The part of you that's grown quiet. Numb. Tired of trying to be okay.

I feel your pain—because I've lived it too.

So, I'm diving in. I want to bring you back to the surface. To help you breathe again. To offer you a second chance at your own life—one where *you* get to be whole, visible, and free.

This is more than just a book about abuse. It's a book about disappearing—and then coming back to life.

While my experience was within a marriage relationship, emotional abuse doesn't only happen between partners or spouses. It can come from parents, siblings, bosses, religious leaders, or friends. It can happen in any relationship where control, manipulation, shame, or silence are used to make you doubt yourself.

This book is written in the voice I know—one shaped by my experience as a woman—but it's for anyone who has ever questioned their reality, carried shame that wasn't theirs, or wondered why love felt like pain. No matter how you identify or where you've been, if these words speak to you, they're for you.

If someone in your life used control, manipulation, shame, or silence to make you doubt yourself, that was emotional abuse—no matter what role they played.

Maybe you're still in a relationship, a family, or a belief system that tells you your pain is your fault. Maybe you've left the relationship—but the damage stayed. Maybe you've spent years blaming yourself for why love hurt so much.

I wrote this because I know what it's like to question your own reality. To carry shame that wasn't yours. To try harder when it only made things worse. To wonder if you're too sensitive or just not strong enough.

This book isn't about blaming. It's about naming. Because once you name the pattern, you can break it. Once you see the truth, you can stop abandoning yourself to survive. Once you begin telling your story, the healing begins.

You don't have to be perfect to be free.

You don't need permission to start over.

You are already enough, even if you don't believe that yet.

This is a survivor's guide—but it's also a reclamation. Of your voice. Your worth. Your power. Of everything you were told to surrender to be loved.

We're not here to survive silently. We're here to come alive.

# PART I

# The Slow Disappearance

*It doesn't start with one big moment.*
*It starts with a thousand small ones—*
*The quiet, unremarkable ways you stop recognizing yourself.*
*In the smiles that don't quite reach your eyes.*
*In constant second-guessing that becomes your inner monologue.*

*It's not just the harm that changes you—it's the way you start adapting to survive it.*
*You downplay your needs. You soften your truth.*
*You twist yourself into shapes just to keep the peace.*
*And at some point, you stop asking if you're okay.*
*You just try harder.*

*I didn't realize I was disappearing.*
*Because on the outside, I looked fine.*
*But underneath the calm exterior, I was unraveling —*
*not all at once, but in a thousand quiet ways.*

*This is where the unraveling began.*
*Where the mask went on.*
*Where I lost my reflection, even while I kept functioning.*
*Where I forget that I had a self to return to.*

*But underneath the silence, a whisper remained —*
*a knowing, a flicker, a question I wasn't ready to ask yet.*

*Is this really love?*
*Or is this the slowest kind of loss?*

*I am ...*

## Chapter 1

# Red Flags and Rose-Colored Glasses

**Red Flags**

It was my wedding day. A day that should have been full of joy, celebration, and love. But it wasn't. Something felt wrong—and deep down, I knew it. We don't always listen to the quiet voice inside us. Sometimes we call it nerves, or timing, or stress. Sometimes we silence it completely, hoping it will go away. I did.

My soon-to-be husband was socially shy—or at least, that's what I told myself. So I agreed to a small wedding. Just the two of us, the minister, and a witness. No family. No friends. No celebration. Why I said yes to that, I still don't fully understand. Maybe I thought I was being flexible. Maybe I didn't want to make a fuss. I was older. It was my second marriage. And maybe, on some level, I already knew something was off.

My first marriage ended after twenty-five years, when my husband decided he'd rather be with his girlfriends than with me. It was devastating. We had built a life together—four amazing children, decades of memories, a shared history. By the time everything fell apart, our kids were grown and living their own lives. But I was still standing there, holding the pieces of a life I thought would last.

Not long after my divorce, I lost my job. I had been teaching at a school I loved—but when the school consolidated and closed, so did that chapter of my life. Teaching wasn't just a job to me. It was my dream. I loved awakening young minds, helping them find their voices. Losing that role felt like losing a part of who I was. Suddenly, the two things that had anchored me—my marriage and my calling—were gone. I had no clear vision of what came next. I was unmoored. Floundering. Grieving more than I could put into words.

The school that absorbed our students failed to absorb any of the teachers. At the time, three of my children were in college, so money was tight. I needed a job—fast. I was hired by a Fortune 500 company, launching me into the corporate world. For someone raised in a small town, someone who had spent her career in the quiet rhythms of a classroom, it was a shock. Everything moved faster. The rules were different. The values were different—louder, harsher, built on power instead of kindness. And deep down, I knew I didn't belong. But instead of walking away, I started adapting. I thought if I could just be flexible, I could make it work. So I began to bend—one compromise at a time—until survival replaced selfhood.

It was in this environment that I met my future second husband. I enjoyed living alone and had a great amount of undisturbed peace. People tried to push me into new relationships, assuming I couldn't be happy alone. But I wasn't lonely. I had friends, family, and responsibilities in the community. I had no intention of getting into a new relationship. *I was fine—or so I thought.*

I met him at work. I wasn't looking, but he was hunting. I hadn't been in the dating game for nearly thirty years. My first husband had been the only relationship I'd ever had. So, when this man from work asked me to have lunch, I said, "Okay, why not?"

## The First Warning

We had lunch in the park. Something felt off. He wanted to eat in a secluded spot—one that was hard to get to and hidden from the road. He kept scanning the area, as if he were looking for someone or something, but I couldn't tell what. He seemed incredibly nervous. None of it was overtly wrong… but it unsettled me. I felt it in my body. Still, I told myself I was overthinking it. I had a good time, so I dismissed the red flag. But that wasn't the last one. One by one, they kept appearing. I thought I was the beginning of something new. But I wasn't. I was a secret.

Our office was thirty-five miles from my home. Once, I got caught in a snowstorm and went by his apartment to wait out the storm. He was still at work and had invited me to endure the storm at his apartment since I had so far to travel, but suddenly he totally freaked out, afraid I would get on his computer. He started calling and texting frantically. I hadn't planned to get on the computer, but his reaction was strange. I didn't say anything at the time, but the way he panicked left a knot in my stomach. I brushed it off—until the truth came out. Later, I discovered his computer was filled with pornography.

He would seclude himself to use his phone and said it was his mom. It wasn't. It was a girlfriend I didn't know about. I found a needle in his bathroom. He claimed it belonged to a friend of his with diabetes. Later, I learned he was using drugs. I ignored each red flag, making excuses, justifying his behavior.

I had ignored every sign. And now, there I was—marrying someone I barely knew, surrounded by silence. And it was like the twilight zone. Why do we do this to ourselves?

## I Know Who I Am

> **Self-Check—Do you listen to red flags?**
>
> Why do we do that to ourselves? Red flags pop up for a reason. Ignoring them often leads to pain.
>
> Here are some reasons why we ignore red flags:
>
> - We doubt our judgment.
> - We fear being alone.
> - We think we can fix them.
> - We fear the red flags are true.
> - We doubt our intuition.
> - We believe relationships are hard work and that we just need to work harder.
> - We don't respect ourselves.
> - We don't believe we deserve better.
> - We are willing to settle.
> - We make excuses for behavior to make things work.
> - We fear starting over.
> - We focus on potential instead of reality.
> - We're indecisive.
> - We're people pleasers.
> - We fear rejection or confrontation.
> - We get stuck in wishful thinking.
>
> Not just once—I've done all of these at some point.

## Ways to Reclaim Yourself

Red flags aren't always obvious, but you can learn to recognize them. The key? Know yourself. Know what you value. Know what you will and won't tolerate. Know that red flags don't go away. They need to be addressed.

Here are ways to spot red flags:

- Trust your body. If something feels off—a gut feeling, a wave of nausea, the urge to run, a nagging thought—pay attention.
- Know your values and boundaries. If you don't know them, how will you know when they're crossed?
- Watch for patterns. Is this a onetime issue or a recurring behavior? Write things down if it helps.
- Pay attention to intuition – that gut feeling, hunch, sensitivity to something. It's there to protect you.
- Learn from the past. If something reminds you of a toxic person from your past, listen to that cue.

You can learn to spot red flags. You can manage difficult situations. You can live in healthy, respectful relationships.

It's okay if this feels hard. The fact that you're here means something in you is ready.

## Say It. Write It. Own It.

*You saw more than you gave yourself credit for. Let this be the place where you start trusting what you knew.*

## Journal Prompt #1:

*Can you remember a moment when something felt "off" early in a relationship—but you dismissed it? What did your body, spirit, or intuition try to tell you at the time?*

## Journal Prompt #2:

*What messages (from childhood, culture, or past experiences) taught you to ignore red flags or minimize discomfort in relationships?*

## Exercise: Create Your Red Flag List

- Write down at least 3 to 5 red flags that you now recognize in past (or current) relationships.

- Next to each one, jot down the **justification** you gave at the time.
- Then, rewrite that justification into the **truth** you would offer your past self now.

## Example:

- Red flag: He got angry when I talked to male friends.
- Old excuse: "He just cares a lot."

- New truth: "That was control disguised as concern. Caring shouldn't come with isolation."

*Red flags aren't redemptive arcs—they're warnings.
You don't need to wait for proof to walk away from harm.*

*I am learning to
see clearly.*

## CHAPTER 2

# When You've Been Taught Not to Trust Yourself

You knew something felt off—but you talked yourself out of it.

When you've been taught to doubt your instincts, trusting yourself can feel impossible.

## The Trap of Doubt

Finding your way forward begins with choosing a path that leads to freedom. I hoped I was stepping into something full of promise. But the road I chose wasn't smooth or safe. It felt more like it was full of rocky cliffs and fiery deserts.

After that first awkward lunch in the park, I didn't pursue anything. But he did. He was persistent. He sent daily emails, dropped by my desk, and found little ways to wedge himself into my world. I felt confused. I hadn't encouraged it, but his attention was constant—and part of me felt flattered. That's where it started: the inner conflict between what I felt and what I thought I should feel. I knew I was being pulled in, and the worst part? I felt helpless to stop it.

Why? Because I didn't know how to say no.

## The Roots of "Yes"

My father was authoritarian. He probably didn't know any better. That's how it was in his childhood, so I grew up under constant control:

"You can't wear that."

"You can't go there."

"You can't think that."

"I'll tell you what to do."

My father came from a generation where men controlled everything: where to go, what to wear, what to think. There was no room for me to develop my own voice. 'No' wasn't part of my vocabulary—it wasn't safe. Safety meant blind submission and obedience. I became a doormat. I followed every rule, jumped when told, ran when pushed. I was trained to comply. I learned to hide and blend in so I wouldn't be easily found.

So when this man—who, by now, had proven himself deceptive—showed up again and said he wanted exclusivity, I didn't protest. Even though we weren't even dating. Even though I wasn't interested. I told myself maybe I'd given him the wrong idea. I didn't ask why he felt entitled to my yes. I just assumed my no hadn't been clear enough. That it was my fault. That I owed him something—for being nice, for showing interest, for not giving up on me. I'd been taught that politeness was a kind of contract, that kindness came with unspoken obligations. Like when the other children at school called me names and I was told not to tattle or retaliate—but to take it and walk away. Being quiet and agreeable was what made you good. So I said yes, not because I wanted to—but because I didn't know I was allowed to say no.

## I didn't trust myself.

I excused his behavior because he "had potential." He had a good job. People liked him. He laughed easily. That had to mean he was kind, right? I told myself to stop resisting and give it a chance.

Wrong decision.

You might wonder how I could've said yes to someone who'd already shown so many red flags. I've wondered that too.

I hoped he was as kind as he seemed—hoped in his potential, in the person I believed he could become.

I was so used to people-pleasing, to looking for the good in others and ignoring the bad. I'd grown up being told what to do. That's what authoritarian fathers do in the name of protection. My first husband was controlling, maybe even narcissistic. I didn't know how to say no.

So I didn't.

## The Spiral

Later I found out—he hadn't broken things off with his girlfriend like he said. In fact, he thought she was pregnant.

So what did he say to me? "What should we do?"

What I should have said: "We? Sir, there is no we."

What I actually said: "People make mistakes. We'll work through this."

OKAY! I hear you. I should've given him the boot. Bye-Bye. Sayonara. Adios. Hasta la vista. Au revoir. Auf Wiedersehen. DaH jlmel. (Don't google that. It's Klingon for good-bye.) Any language would have done the job.

But I didn't. I said nothing.

At that point, I had invested so much in the relationship, and I didn't want to start over. I didn't want to admit I'd chosen wrong.

What I failed to see was that he hadn't invested anything at all.

He was dishonest, distracted, and distant—but I kept trying to fix what he never intended to build.

Why didn't I walk away? Because I didn't trust myself to make good decisions. My first marriage had ended in betrayal. I felt like I had failed even though it wasn't me who was the betrayer. So now, I assumed I couldn't judge people accurately.

That thinking was poison.

I eventually ended the relationship. I asked him not to contact me again. He respected that—briefly. But a few months later, he showed up at my doorstep with bags in hand. He claimed he'd had a vision—I was "the one," and he couldn't live without me.

And just like that—he moved in. Uninvited. Unwelcome. Because I didn't know how to say no.

I didn't want him there, but self-doubt silenced me—I couldn't say it out loud.

I didn't trust myself—to be right, to say no, to stand on my own *at all*.

Everyone else seemed to like him. Had they seen something I didn't? Was it possible I was overreacting? Maybe I was wrong—again.

So, I stayed silent. I second-guessed. I deferred to him.

And then one day... we were married. I said no a dozen times. He asked a dozen more. Eventually, he planned the wedding himself, and one Saturday, I just got in the car and went along with it.

I cried the entire day. Quietly, constantly. Not out of joy or nerves—but something heavier. I wasn't even sure what to call it. All I knew was that something in me was breaking. I felt trapped in a story I hadn't written, playing a role I never agreed to.

I didn't want to do it. But by then, I didn't even know what I wanted anymore. He had been deciding for me for so long—what I liked, what I felt, what I needed—that my own voice felt like a distant echo.

I told myself it was easier to just go along with it. But deep down, I knew: I wasn't saying yes. I was giving up. I was abandoning myself to avoid the storm I knew would come if I didn't comply. And that's why I cried—because some part of me knew I'd just disappeared.

### Self-Check: Do You Trust Yourself?

When you've spent years doubting your own voice, it can look like this:

- You're terrified of making the wrong decision.
- You delay decisions, hoping someone else will make them for you.
- You feel guilty after making choices.
- You constantly seek validation from others.
- You believe other people's opinions more than your own.
- You can't identify your own needs or preferences.
- You apologize for asking for anything.
- You second-guess everything—even your favorite color.
- You ask three people before making even a small decision.
- You don't believe you're enough on your own.

If any of that sounds familiar, I want you to know: **you're not alone. And you're not broken. You can unlearn this. You can rebuild.**

## Ways to Reclaim Yourself

Rebuilding trust in yourself takes time, but it starts with small steps:

- **Be you.** Even if you're not sure who that is yet. Start small. Find one thing that feels true—and honor it without apology or fear of judgment.

- **Be kind to yourself.** Accept who you are and give yourself a little grace—eat the chocolate.
- **Stop apologizing for existing.** You don't need to justify your feelings or choices. Don't let your inner critic have that kind of power.
- **Make small decisions daily.** Practice trusting yourself in low-risk ways. Choose what to eat. Pick a show to watch. Learn what you like.
- **Be decisive.** As you grow in making small decisions, learn to trust your inner compass and follow your values.
- **Set realistic goals.** It's ok to aim high but make sure the goals are attainable.
- **Visualize positive outcomes.** Stop fixating on what could go wrong. Start imagining what could go right.
- **Live in the present.** When your mind races to the past or the future, come back to this moment. Breathe. Notice your surroundings. Notice what's happening in you—right here, right now. This is where healing begins.
- **Build on your strengths.** Find what you are good at and focus on that.
- **Get support.** Build a tribe that reminds you of your strength, not your weakness.
- **Celebrate wins.** Even small victories are signs you're learning to lead your own life.
- **Affirm your worth.** Say it out loud: "I can trust myself. I know what I need."

You are capable. You are learning to trust your wisdom. You are resilient. You don't have to know everything. You just have to believe that your voice matters—starting now.

## Say It. Write It. Own It.

*Learning to trust yourself again takes time—but reflection is how you begin rebuilding the bridge back to your voice.*

## Journal Prompt #1:

*In what ways have you silenced your own voice to keep the peace? Write about a time when you ignored your gut instinct—and what happened as a result.*

## Journal Prompt #2:

*What messages did you receive (in childhood, religion, relationships, or society) that made you doubt your own judgment? Whose voice lives in your head when you're second-guessing yourself?*

## Exercise: Rebuilding the Bridge to You

### Step 1: Notice Where It Started
- List three ways you've learned not to trust yourself (e.g., "I always ask others before making decisions," "I feel guilty when I say no," "I assume I'm wrong.").

### Step 2: Interrupt the Pattern
- For each item, write a possible **reframe**—a small affirmation or truth that could interrupt that habit.

### Example:
- Old pattern: "I always second-guess my decisions."
- Reframe: "Every time I choose, I'm thinking it through—and trusting myself to decide what's best for me."

### Step 3: Take One Small Action Today
- Make one tiny, deliberate decision today—just for you.
  - What to eat.
  - What to wear.
  - Whether to rest or move.
  - Who to say no to.
- Then **write down how it felt**. Was it easy? Hard? Did you feel proud, scared, guilty, free?

*Healing begins with one small,  
self-honoring choice at a time.  
You don't have to be fearless to start.  
You just have to begin.*

*I am reclaiming my intuition.*

# Chapter 3

# Please Hold While I Disappear

I stood in the kitchen, staring at the dinner I had just cooked. He hadn't said thank you. He hadn't said anything. I don't know why I expected him to. I moved around him like furniture—quiet, unnoticed, necessary. I didn't ask how his day was. I didn't ask for help. I didn't ask anything at all. I could feel the silence settling over me like dust, like maybe I wasn't even there anymore. Just a shadow holding a spoon. I remember thinking: When did I stop being someone?

When truth keeps getting dismissed, the urge to speak it fades. The fight to be heard begins to feel pointless. Bit by bit, presence dims—slowly, quietly, and on purpose.

## When You Can't Hear Your Own Voice

There's a slow fade that happens when you're in an emotionally abusive relationship. It's not always a crash—it's a quiet erosion.

At first, you give up little things.

Your preferences.

Your routines.

Your opinions.

That color you loved gets pushed to the back of the closet because he made a face when you wore it. The ringtone that used to make you smile gets changed without a second thought—it annoyed him anyway. Phone calls with close friends happen less and less. There's always a reason, a raised eyebrow, a subtle dig that makes it easier not to bother.

I remember once putting on a favorite scarf—bold, colorful, a gift from someone who really saw me. He looked at me, smirked, and said, "You're not seriously wearing that, are you?"

I laughed it off. Took it off. Never wore it again. I never wore any scarf again. It felt small in the moment. But it chipped away at something sacred.

You think you're compromising. But underneath it all, something quieter is happening: You're beginning to fade.

## The Disappearing Act

I didn't wake up one morning and say, "You know what, I'd love to lose my identity today."

But it happened anyway.

I became isolated. First emotionally, then socially. I couldn't talk to my friends the way I used to. I started filtering what I said to him, afraid it would be repeated, twisted, or used against me later. He never said, "Don't talk to them." He didn't have to. He just made it clear they weren't safe—because they asked too many questions, saw too much, or reminded me of who I used to be.

So, I stayed silent and stopped asking for what I needed. Eventually, the feelings numbed—because numbness felt easier than constant disappointment. Little by little, I began to disappear—to him, and eventually, to myself. I didn't just stop feeling. I went invisible. I disappeared into the background of my own life.

## Signs You Might Be Losing Yourself

If you're not sure whether this is happening to you, here are some signs:

- You feel like you're walking on eggshells.
- You second-guess your thoughts and feelings constantly.
- Your friendships fade.
- You feel guilty for having boundaries.
- Your world revolves around them.
- You forget what you even like anymore.
- Your hobbies slip away.
- Your future revolves around them, not anything you want or need.
- You don't recognize yourself in the mirror.
- You're emotionally exhausted—but you can't explain why.
- You're not even your own priority.
- You're the one apologizing.
- You find yourself feeling anxious more often.
- You realize your thoughts revolve around the relationship—even when you're not in it.
- It's you who are the one that's willing to change.
- You fantasize about leaving—but feel paralyzed.

This isn't drama. It isn't "just a hard patch." This is what it feels like to lose yourself.

## The Turning Point

I remember exactly when the realization hit. It happened during a conversation with some ladies discussing repainting some rooms in their home. As they tossed around color choices, one of them turned and asked for my opinion. Panic surged. Not because I was shy—but because I didn't have one. Somewhere along the way, even preferences had vanished.

Another memory still haunts me: standing in my closet, staring at clothes I didn't even like anymore, realizing I couldn't name a single thing that felt like me. Somewhere along the way, my colors had gone quiet, my choices had gone missing, and even my preferences had vanished. In that moment—mid-stare, mid-loss—something inside me snapped. I looked around and thought, *"Who is this woman?"*

There was no recognition.

That moment didn't give me the courage to make a sudden change—but it planted a seed.

And from that seed, something slowly, stubbornly, began to grow.

---

### Self-Check: Are You Starting to Disappear?

When survival becomes your daily rhythm, the signs of disappearing often feel subtle—until they don't. Let's do a little check and see if parts of you have been fading.

- Have I stopped expressing certain opinions, styles, or emotions to avoid conflict?
- Do I feel smaller, quieter, or less visible than I used to?
- Am I afraid to ask for what I need—or do I believe I shouldn't need anything at all?
- Do I avoid talking to friends or family because it feels easier not to explain?
- Can I remember what I love, what I want, or who I am—outside of this relationship?
- Do I feel like I'm fading from my own life?

If any of this feels familiar, please hear this: fading from yourself was never a failure. It was a response to pain. And you don't have to stay hidden. You're still here—and your return begins with one small act of self-honoring at a time.

## Ways to Reclaim Yourself

You don't just "get yourself back" after abuse. You rebuild. One brick at a time. Here's how I started:

### 1. Reconnect With Your Inner Voice
- I filled notepads and journals—just to hear myself think again.
- I read books about emotional abuse and realized—I wasn't the one confused or imagining things.
- I visualized my future in small, honest pieces.
- I searched for my purpose.
- I learned to say "No."

### 2. Restore Your Daily Life
- I set realistic goals, no matter how small they seemed.
- I made one brave choice a day: say no, speak up, go for a walk, eat what I wanted.
- I began creating healthy boundaries.
- I practiced living in the moment.
- I decluttered my space.
- I made sure to get enough sleep.
- I did things I enjoyed.
- I took time for self-care.

### 3. Rebuild Safe Connection
- I spent time alone on purpose—not in isolation, but in restoration.
- I reconnected with friends.
- I asked for help—even when it felt humiliating.
- I built support systems that reminded me of my strength.

It wasn't instant or easy. But it was possible. And it started the moment I said: "I deserve to exist as myself."

You deserve to exist as yourself, too.

## Say It. Write It. Own It.

*You don't have to stay invisible. Naming what you've lost is how you begin reclaiming who you are.*

## Journal Prompt #1:

*What parts of yourself did you stop expressing to "keep the peace"? Think about the way you dressed, talked, felt, believed, or dreamed. What parts of you grew quiet or slipped away?*

## Journal Prompt #2:

*When did you first realize you no longer recognized yourself? What did that moment feel like—emotionally, physically, spiritually?*

## Exercise: Remembering Who You Are

### Step 1: Reclaim Your "Before"
- Write a list of 5-10 things you loved, enjoyed, or felt passionate about before this relationship.
  - These could be hobbies, places, types of people, books, dreams—anything that felt like *you*.

**Step 2: Name What's Missing Now**
- Circle the things you've abandoned or forgotten. Ask: *Why did I stop? Who was I trying to protect? What did I fear would happen if I kept being that version of myself?*

**Step 3: Take a Small Step Toward One Thing**
- Choose one circled item and commit to a small act that reconnects you to it.
  - If it was painting—buy a set of paints.
  - If it was laughter—watch something silly.
  - If it was nature—go outside barefoot.
- Write how it felt. Even if it was uncomfortable or bittersweet, that's okay. The goal isn't instant joy—it's *re-entry*.

*You are not lost. You are layered.*
*And every layer you peel back*
*brings you closer to the real you.*

*I am reconnecting with an old friend —me.*

## Chapter 4

# Shrinking Was How I Survived

I remember standing in front of my closet, full of dark clothes. Where were the bright colors and bold patterns I used to love—pieces that used to feel like "me"? The only color left was the bright pink he wanted me to wear, so I'd "look more like a girl." I reached in and pulled out a black top to go with the black pants. I didn't realize I was disappearing from my own life, one compromise at a time.

It wasn't just my wardrobe that changed. He used to say, "You used to look so good," like I was some fading version of someone I'd failed to keep being.

One night, I was frying chicken when the grease popped and burned my face. It stung—sharp, hot, terrifying. But instead of helping, he looked at me and said, "I can't be with someone whose face could be disfigured." He didn't ask if I was okay. He didn't bring me an ice pack or take me to the hospital. He didn't do any of those things. What he did was strip me of my humanity in one sentence, reducing me to a face instead of a person.

It wasn't just that moment. He always had something to say about my hair, too. It was never right. Never enough. And eventually, I stopped trying. I stopped dressing like myself. I stopped expecting kindness. I stopped looking in the mirror with kindness.

That's what body shaming does. It strips you down until you forget who you were before the shame settled in. You don't just lose your reflection—you start to lose your self-worth.

By the time I noticed how far I'd shrunk, it felt like there was no room left for me.

Disappearing wasn't accidental—it was survival. I didn't just fade. I folded. I made myself smaller, quieter, easier to love, because it felt safer that way.

I stopped ordering what I really wanted at restaurants—just picked something cheap and simple so I wouldn't seem difficult. I turned down invitations because he didn't like the people who invited me. I stopped laughing too loud. I avoided wearing makeup or bright lipstick because he said it made me look "fake." Even in the way I sat—legs tucked, arms crossed, eyes down—I was trying to take up less space.

## I Didn't Just Lose Myself—I Made Myself Smaller

I didn't stop being me all at once. I shrank in pieces. A little less volume. A little more hesitation. A careful edit here. A swallowed truth there. It didn't feel like self-abandonment at the time. It felt like safety.

I stopped wearing the colors I loved—swapping bold patterns for black, or the bright pink he insisted on, even though I hated it. I stopped sharing my dreams and ideas, afraid they'd be dismissed or twisted. I stopped laughing out loud. I stopped taking up space. Little by little, I shrank—to fit into the version of me that made him comfortable.

I wasn't being silenced—I was silencing myself. Because I thought that way, maybe it would hurt less. If I stayed quiet, agreeable, invisible—maybe I could avoid the next wave of blame or ridicule. Maybe I could avoid the next explosion, the next accusation, the next cold silence. I got rid of clothes I loved because he didn't like them. I stopped cooking food I liked because he wouldn't eat it. I only went for walks when he was sleeping, because even that simple act of peace felt like something I had to hide. But the truth is, it still hurt. I just blamed myself for it instead.

## Shrinking Felt Like Love

I thought I was showing kindness. I let things go. I didn't bring up what hurt me because I didn't want to seem too sensitive. When he asked me to invite some people we knew to dinner, I said yes—even though I was tired and anxious. But when they arrived, he locked himself in the bedroom and never came down. I made excuses for him all night.

I thought I was being flexible. I adjusted to his moods. I went alone to holiday dinners and family birthdays so no one would feel uncomfortable—even though I felt humiliated and heartbroken every time he refused to come. Even when they were in our home.

I changed my plans, my preferences, even my values to avoid conflict. I stopped reading books and listening to music. I canceled vacation plans. I stopped eating food I liked. And of course—there was the pink.

I thought I was being easy to love. I worked hard to make sure he was okay—even when I wasn't. But all that bending never made him kinder. It only made me disappear.

I thought if I could just be smaller—less dramatic, less emotional, less "difficult"—I'd finally be enough.

For him.

I remember quietly choking back tears because I didn't want to upset him. I smiled a weak smile instead. I said I was fine—everything was fine.

It wasn't fine.

Nothing was fine.

I didn't realize I was disappearing.

## The Lies That Taught Me to Shrink

I didn't invent this behavior. I inherited it. Somewhere along the way, mostly when I was a child, I learned:

- Don't make waves.
- Don't take up too much space.

- Don't speak until spoken to.
- Don't be too emotional.
- Don't be "a lot."
- Don't make people uncomfortable.
- Don't outshine anyone.
- Don't say no—it's rude.
- Don't need too much—you'll drive people away.
- Don't ask for help—you'll look weak.
- Don't be angry—it's ugly.
- Don't question authority—it makes you difficult.
- Don't be too confident—it's arrogant.
- Don't cry—it makes people uncomfortable.
- Don't tell the truth if it might upset someone.

So I made myself **less** to be loved **more**.

## The Things I Stopped Doing

I didn't even notice how much I'd lost—until one day, someone asked me what I liked to do for fun… and I couldn't answer. I stared at them, blank. Not because I didn't want to respond—but because I honestly didn't know. I'd spent so long catering to someone else's wants, shrinking to fit his moods, that I had no idea what brought me joy anymore. I had traded my preferences for false peace so many times, I didn't remember what I enjoyed. I didn't remember me.

That question haunted me. What did I like to do? So I started to trace my way back—to remember the things I had set down along the way.

- Laughing too loud
- Dressing how I wanted
- Speaking my opinions
- Taking up time

# Shrinking Was How I Survived

- Asking questions
- Being seen
- Needing anything
- Reading books
- Listening to music I liked
- Telling the truth if it might start a fight
- Making decisions without checking first
- Celebrating myself (just in case it looked like bragging)
- Saying "I don't like that"
- Dreaming out loud
- Wishing out loud
- Believing I could have more

I stopped being *me* in order to stay *safe*.

## But Shrinking Didn't Protect Me—It Just Erased Me

No matter how careful I was, I still got hurt. No matter how small I became, it still wasn't small enough. Because shrinking didn't stop the pain. It just numbed me to it.

**I thought making myself easier to love would make me safer. All it made me was invisible.**

### I'm Not Doing That Anymore

Now, I know:

- I don't have to earn space.
- I don't have to be less to be worthy.
- I don't have to filter my feelings to be lovable.

I'm allowed to take up space. To speak up. To need things. To be big. To be *whole*.

Shrinking was survival. But now, I'm choosing something else: **returning.**

Returning to my voice.
Returning to my body.
Returning to my instincts.

Returning to my spirit.
Returning to the woman I was always meant to be.

Returning to the person I always believed I could be.

I'm not trying to become someone new. I'm coming back to someone I never should've had to leave behind.

> ### Self-Check: Are You Still Shrinking to Survive?
>
> Shrinking often doesn't look like pain. It looks like politeness, perfection, silence, or "just being easy to be around." But here's how to tell if you're still disappearing in plain sight.
>
> - You downplay your emotions, so others won't feel uncomfortable.
> - You constantly second-guess how you come across.
> - You hesitate to share good news because you don't want to seem "too proud."
> - You speak softly, even when you have something important to say.
> - You apologize when you have done nothing wrong.
> - You instinctively defer to others, even when you have an opinion.
> - You get anxious when someone asks, "What do you want?"

- You tell yourself, *"It's not a big deal,"* even when it is.
- You try to be "low maintenance" so no one ever leaves you.
- You feel safest when you're invisible.

You didn't shrink because you were weak. Shrinking happened because that's what the world taught you to do to stay safe. But you're allowed to take up space now. All of it.

## Ways to Reclaim Yourself

You don't have to roar to reclaim your space. You just have to stop apologizing for taking up the room you already belong in.

- Take up more *physical* space today: sit with your shoulders back, wear something bold, stretch, move freely. Let your body feel presence.
- Say something out loud that you've been keeping inside. Even if it's just to yourself.
- Practice this response when someone asks what you want: *"Let me think about what I want—because that matters."*
- Stop softening your voice in emails, texts, or conversations. Delete the "just checking," "sorry to bother," or "I might be wrong, but…"
- Choose something *just* for you today: your food, your music, your way. No compromises this time.
- Name one way you've made yourself smaller—and do the opposite.

You're not too much. You're just finally not pretending to be less.

## Say It. Write It. Own It.

*Shrinking helped you survive—but writing is where you start to expand again. This is where you take yourself off mute.*

## Journal Prompt #1:

*When did you first learn that having needs wasn't safe? What happened the first time you took up space and someone made you feel small for it?*

## Journal Prompt #2:

*What parts of yourself have you been keeping small—on purpose or without even realizing it? What would it look like to let one of those parts breathe again?*

## Exercise: Reverse the Shrinking

### Step 1: Track the Silence
Write a list of moments when you recently made yourself smaller. It might sound like:

- "I didn't speak up when I disagreed."
- "I let someone interrupt me—and didn't return to my point."
- "I wore something safe instead of something that felt like me."

**Step 2: Speak the Reversal**

Next to each, write what you *wish* you'd done or said.
Then choose one—and do it today.
Say it. Wear it. Own it.

**Step 3: Write This Out Loud**

Finish the sentence:
*"Today, I take up space by…"*
Do it every morning this week. Make it a ritual of return.

*You were never a burden.*
*They just weren't ready for*
*your full volume. But you are.*
*And that's what matters.*

*I am
unapologetically
here.*

## Interlude

# The Good That Kept Me

It wasn't always bad.

That's the part people don't see when they ask, *"Why did you stay?"* They see the broken parts. The bruised parts. The unraveling.

They don't see the small moments that felt like safety. The days that felt like connection. The nights where I almost believed we'd make it.

There was good.

And that good kept me.

He could be charming. He could be kind. He made me laugh when no one else could. He told me I was amazing when I was falling apart. He held me close—just long enough to confuse my fear with love.

And for a while, I believed the good outweighed the bad. That the bad was temporary. Fixable. *My fault.* And if it was my fault, I thought I could fix it.

It wasn't always bad—but it was never safe for my heart, never honest, never whole. And that's what I didn't know then.

**The good doesn't erase the harm.**
**The harm doesn't make the good a lie.**
**But the good doesn't make the harm less true.**

It was the good that kept me. Until it wasn't good enough anymore. And then, something shifted.

I stopped chasing the good. I started listening to the pain. And that's when the real work began.

*I am grateful
and growing.*

## Chapter 5

# Disappearing Into the Background

I remember sitting on the edge of my bed, holding my phone, trying to think of someone to call—and realizing there wasn't anyone I could. Not because they weren't there, but because I had stopped being someone who reached out.

I got so good at blending into the background that eventually, no one came looking for me. And the worst part? I didn't even notice I was alone—until I already was.

## Isolation Doesn't Always Happen All at Once

No one told me I was being isolated. There wasn't a dramatic moment where I was cut off from the world. It was slower. Softer. Easier to justify.

A text left unanswered here. A plan canceled last-minute there. A friendship that started to feel too complicated to maintain. A subtle pressure to spend all my time with him. And I went along with it—because I thought that's what love looked like.

What I didn't realize was that love doesn't demand your world shrink to fit someone else's comfort. That's not connection. That's control.

## It Started with Little Things

It didn't begin with some dramatic moment. It began with quiet compromises—little things I gave up to avoid conflict.

- I stopped calling friends because he got moody when I did.
- I stopped making plans because I didn't want to deal with the questions.
- I stopped sharing details with family because I didn't want to defend my choices.
- I stopped asking for help because I didn't want anyone to know what was really going on.

And slowly, my circle got smaller. Not just physically—but emotionally. I didn't notice it shrinking until I looked around—and no one was there.

I was surrounded by people… but no one really *knew* me anymore. Not even me.

## Isolation Wasn't Always Forced—Sometimes I Did It to Myself

That's the hardest part to admit. Because if I chose it, that means I could've stopped it. Right? But it's not that simple. Sometimes self-isolation is the only safe option we can find.

It didn't always feel like I was being pushed away. Sometimes it felt like I was choosing peace by avoiding the people who might challenge me. But peace and silence are not the same thing. And now I know—I wasn't at peace. I was alone. And not by accident.

## You Don't Realize You're Dissolving Into Silence Until It's Quiet

There comes a moment when you need someone—and no one's there. Or worse, you stop believing anyone *would* be there, even if you asked.

That's what abuse does. It isolates you, not just from your people—but from your voice, your instincts, your reality.

**I Thought I Was Keeping the Peace. I Was Really Keeping the Secret.**

The silence wasn't safety. It was survival. But I'm not surviving anymore. I'm reconnecting. Reaching out. Letting people in—slowly, honestly, bravely.

I'm building a new kind of community. I'm building my tribe. One where I don't have to disappear to belong.

I didn't know how alone I was until I tried to come back. And now? I know I'm not meant to heal in isolation. And I'm not disappearing anymore.

---

### Self-Check: Are You Isolated—Even If It Doesn't Look Like It?

Isolation in abusive relationships often doesn't feel like being pushed—it feels like slowly stepping away from yourself and your world. Here's what it might look like.

- You've stopped reaching out to friends because it feels exhausting or "not worth it."
- You often think, *"They wouldn't understand anyway."*
- You downplay what's really going on when people ask how you're doing.
- You feel disconnected even when surrounded by people.
- You no longer trust your support system—or you don't think you deserve one.
- You've convinced yourself you prefer being alone—but it feels more like numbness than peace.

> - You feel ashamed of what you've been through, so you stay silent.
> - You tell yourself, *"I don't want to be a burden."*
>
> Isolation isn't always someone else's idea. Sometimes, it's what happens when you don't feel safe being seen.

## Ways to Reclaim Yourself

You don't have to go from invisible to outspoken overnight. Reconnection starts in quiet, honest ways. Let this be your return.

- Reach out to one person who makes you feel safe. You don't have to explain everything. Just start with, *"Hey, I've been thinking about you."*
- Begin telling the truth in small doses. Start with: *"Actually, things have been hard."*
- Say yes to one invite this week—even if it feels awkward. Let your nervous system relearn what community feels like.
- Create a "circle of safety" list: 3–5 people you can reach out to for support, laughter, or truth.
- Remind yourself: *"I'm allowed to be known. I'm allowed to be supported. I'm allowed to come back."*
- Make space for someone else to see you today—and let them.

You don't need a huge circle. You just need a few people who see you fully—and let you stay big.

## Say It. Write It. Own It.

*Letting yourself be seen doesn't mean telling everything. It means slowly, bravely returning to yourself as you step into the light.*

## Journal Prompt #1:

*When did you start pulling away from others? Was it your choice—or something you were taught to do to keep the peace?*

## Journal Prompt #2:

*What's one thing you wish someone had said to you when you felt the most alone? Write it now—and let it be a message to your past self.*

## Exercise: Practice Being Seen

### Step 1: Write It for You
Write a letter to someone in your life you've withdrawn from (you don't have to send it). Be honest. Share why you pulled away. Say what you wish they had known.

## Step 2: Say It Out Loud
Choose a sentence from that letter that feels brave and true. Practice saying it out loud, to yourself in the mirror.
Example:
*"I didn't disappear because I stopped caring. I disappeared because I didn't feel safe."*

## Step 3: Rebuild Gently
Commit to one act of reconnection this week—text, walk, call, journal, post, pray, show up. Let it be imperfect. Let it be real.

*You are not a burden.*
*You are not too much.*
*You are just someone who*
*deserves to belong again.*

*I am changing
my world just
by being myself.*

## Chapter 6

# The Lies I Told Myself to Keep Loving Them

Time and time again, I see myself sitting there—trying to relax after a long day at work—only to come home to cleaning, cooking, and silence. I watched him turn his back on me without a word, my chest tight with shame as he disappeared upstairs and locked himself in the bedroom. I told myself it wasn't that bad. I told myself he was just stressed, or tired, or hurting. I told myself I was fine.

The more alone I felt, the harder I worked to justify it. I kept making excuses, rewriting the story, bending reality to protect the illusion that I was okay.

### I Didn't Want to See It for What It Was

I didn't want to admit I was in something abusive. So, I did what many of us do when we're trying to survive the unbearable:

I tried to make it make sense, justifying it by calling it stress. I'd shrug and say "That's just how men are."

I carried the pain calling myself difficult. Emotional. High maintenance. Then convinced myself that love was supposed to be hard. When it hurt, I told myself that meant I was still fighting for it.

I didn't want to see the spending for what it was, either. Financial abuse doesn't always look like someone locking down the money or cutting off access. Sometimes it looks like one person spending freely—on hobbies, clothes, or status symbols—while ignoring the impact. I'd ask him how we would pay the bills, and instead of considering the situation, he would lock himself away for days.

Meanwhile, I wasn't allowed new clothes. I didn't have a hobby. I felt guilty for spending $10 on myself. Somehow, I ended up carrying all the stress while he spent freely. That's financial abuse, too. It's not just about control—it's about whose needs matter and whose don't.

## I Bargained With My Own Pain

*"He's not always like this."*
*"He's been through a lot."*
*"It's not that bad."*
*"I'm strong—I can handle this."*
*"It'll get better once this season is over."*
*"Maybe I overreacted."*
*"He loves me, he just doesn't know how to show it."*
*"Everyone has problems. Ours are just private."*

I tried to fix it instead of face it. I tried to hold it together instead of let it fall apart. I tried to be good enough to make the bad go away. And all of it kept me stuck.

## I Was Protecting the Hope More Than Myself

The truth is, I didn't want to walk away. I wanted it to get better. I wanted the person I met at the beginning. The good days. The laughter. The spark.

I wanted to believe that version still existed. That the bad was just a phase. So, I ignored the pattern—for almost two decades. I clung to potential. I tried to solve it like a puzzle—one where I was always the missing piece.

But no matter how much I gave, it didn't get better.

## Hope Can Be a Beautiful Thing—Until It Becomes a Trap

Hope kept me in. It made me patient when I needed to be done. It made me forgiving when I needed to be honest. It made me resilient in a situation where I wasn't meant to endure, but to let go.

**I confused loyalty with love.**
**I confused endurance with strength.**
**I confused suffering with meaning.**

## I Don't Need to Make It Make Sense Anymore

It didn't happen because I was broken. It didn't keep happening because I failed to fix it. It happened because someone chose to treat me with less than love.

And now, I don't need another reason. I don't need to explain it to anyone. I don't even need to explain it to myself.

**It was wrong. That's enough. I'm allowed to stop carrying a burden that isn't mine.**

---

### Self-Check: Are You Still Trying to Make It Make Sense?

Bargaining with emotional abuse doesn't always sound like "I deserve this." It often sounds like logic, hope, or compassion. But here's how to know if you're still making excuses for someone else's harm.

- You tell yourself *"It's not that bad"*—even when you know it is.
- You've explained their behavior using their trauma, stress, or past.
- You believe if you could just be more patient, it might change.
- You've said *"every relationship has problems"*—even when it's one-sided.
- You downplay what's happening, so others won't judge you.
- You believe it's your job to fix it, heal it, or hold it together.
- You cling to the "good moments" as proof that it's still worth it.
- You tell yourself it's just a phase—even though the pattern has been years long.
- You feel responsible for their emotions and reactions.

You don't have to prove the pain was real. You only have to stop justifying the reason you stayed.

## Ways to Reclaim Yourself

Letting go of bargaining doesn't mean giving up—it means getting honest. You don't need a reason big enough to choose yourself. You just need a reason *not* to stay.

- Write down every excuse or justification you've used to explain away their behavior. Then ask: *"If a friend told me this, would I believe them?"*

- Practice replacing *"It's not that bad"* with *"It's bad enough that I'm hurting."*
- Make a "truth" column: What is real now? Not what *might* happen—what *is* happening.
- Stop waiting for things to get worse to validate your decision to heal —or to make a different choice.
- Speak this to yourself out loud:

*"I don't need to stay in something just because I hoped it would become something else."*

Hope is beautiful. Hope is necessary. But sometimes, the most loving thing you can do is stop hoping someone will be who they're not.

## Say It. Write It. Own It.

*You've carried the weight of what you hoped it could be. Now let's tell the truth about what it actually was.*

## Journal Prompt #1:

*What's a story you've told yourself to justify staying or surviving in a painful relationship? Where did that story come from—and what do you know now that challenges it?*

## Journal Prompt #2:

*What would it feel like to stop explaining, fixing, or forgiving your way through someone else's harm? What would your life look like if you stopped needing it to make sense?*

## Exercise: Break the Loop

### Step 1: Name the Bargain
Write down the biggest emotional bargain you've made.
Example: *"If I love him enough, he'll stop hurting me."*

### Step 2: Speak the Truth
Write the truth that breaks the loop.
Example: *"I loved him. He still hurt me. That was never mine to fix."*

### Step 3: Write Your Exit Line
Finish this sentence:
**"I don't need this to make sense to walk away. I need _____."**
Let that be your new anchor.

*You tried to make it make sense because you're a good person. Now you get to let go—because you're a free one.*

# *I am telling myself the truth.*

# PART II

# The Truth Starts Speaking

*The truth doesn't shout at first.*
*It whispers. It tugs. It unsettles.*
*It comes in waves—sometimes as doubt, sometimes as rage, sometimes as a quiet ache that says: this isn't okay.*
*You try to silence it. You rationalize. You reframe.*
*You call it stress. A rough patch. Your fault.*
*But the truth is patient. It waits. It circles back.*
*And eventually, it gets louder.*

*This is the part where your inner voice starts to stir.*
*You don't know what to trust yet—except the ache that says something is wrong.*
*Where you begin to name what you couldn't name before.*
*Where the fog doesn't fully lift, but you start seeing shapes in it.*

*You start to realize: the rules keep changing. The stories don't line up.*
*The love feels conditional. The blame always lands on you.*
*And beneath the confusion is clarity—quiet, terrifying, true.*
*This section isn't about breaking free in the way others might expect.*

I Know Who I Am

*It's about breaking silence, breaking self-doubt—*
*hearing yourself again and trusting your own truth.*
*It's the moment you stop gaslighting yourself and begin honoring your knowing.*
*You don't have all the answers.*
*But the silence has been broken.*
*And the truth? Can be silenced no more.*

## Chapter 7

# The Rules Keep Changing

There were so many moments when I would ask a simple question or try to lighten the mood with a joke. His face would change instantly—his eyes would grow dark. What started as a calm conversation would turn into an accusation, and suddenly I was the one apologizing again. I couldn't figure out what I did wrong—only that peace was always one misstep away.

Just when you think you understand how to stay safe, the rules shift again. And every shift teaches you the same lesson: you'll never get it "right" enough to earn peace.

## Confusion Is the First Weapon

Abuse doesn't always come in fists or screaming. Sometimes it comes wrapped in silence. In smiles. In a sweet voice that asks, *"What's wrong with you?"* when you finally speak up.

At first, everything seemed fine—better than fine. He was generous. Attentive. He wanted to know everything about me. I mistook it for interest. But it wasn't curiosity. It was data collection.

He wasn't listening to connect. He was listening to control.

Confusion isn't just emotional—it can be physical, too. Night after night, he'd get up in the middle of the night, flipping on lights, rifling through drawers, banging closet doors, turning on loud music as he got ready for a workout. It was two in the morning. I was exhausted. But I stayed silent. I didn't feel like I was allowed to complain.

Sleep deprivation doesn't always come with threats. Sometimes, it comes with excuses. It's framed as someone else's routine, someone else's right. And when you're too tired to think straight but still expected to keep the peace, you start to question whether your needs even matter. That's not just inconsiderate. That's control disguised as normal life.

Control can show up in what gets broken, too. There was a dent in the wall from his fist. Closet doors that never rolled right because he yanked them off track. Dishes smashed in anger. The car damaged from reckless decisions. Once, he threw a piece of apple pie so hard it hit a picture frame, slammed into the wall, leaving a dent and took the paint off. I used to clean up the messes, patch the holes, pretend it was just stress. But those weren't accidents—they were messages. Not always loud, but clear: Look what I'm capable of. He never had to say the threat out loud. The damage said it for him.

## When Control Pretends to Be Protection

Sometimes control doesn't look like control at all. It dresses up as "concern" or "care." He called it protecting me. But what it really did was isolate me.

I remember once, we were in the city and stopped for gas. I was driving while he slept in the passenger seat. As I got out to pump gas, a man walked by the pump—not saying a word, just walking by. Suddenly, he jumped out of the car, rushed to my side, and got between me and the stranger. He called me "my woman" like I was property. It wasn't about safety. It was about ownership.

Then there was the time I was out with women from my church, painting ceramics—just a simple, peaceful night with friends. He started sending dozens of texts accusing me of cheating, saying he wanted a divorce. The church event was all over social media. Everyone knew where I was. But that wasn't the point. The point was control.

Overprotecting isn't about keeping you safe—it's about making you feel watched. Owned. Guilty for having a life beyond him.

## Control Isn't Always Obvious

I didn't notice the control at first because it didn't look like what I expected. It wasn't "Do what I say!" It was:

- "Are you really going to wear that?"
- "You're so perfect."
- "I'm just trying to help."
- "You must be stressed out."
- "No one else would put up with you, you know."
- "Your friends are not good people."
- "You're remembering it wrong. I never did that."
- "Why are you always so defensive?"
- "You have no reason to be upset."
- "You know I was joking."
- "You are mine and only mine."
- "You don't love me if you don't do this."
- "I know what you're thinking."
- "You read too much into things."
- "You're taking this too seriously."

Every disagreement became a courtroom scene—and I was always on trial.

## When Watching Isn't About Safety

There's a difference between caring where someone is—and tracking them to maintain control. Healthy concern sounds like, *"Let me know you got home safe."* One winter weekend, I drove my daughter back to the Naval Academy—four hours there, four hours home—through freezing rain and blowing snow. She had to be back on time, and I had no choice but to push through the ice and exhaustion alone. Not once did he call to check on me. When I got home, he was sound asleep. He didn't care whether I made it home safely. That wasn't the kind of watching he did.

Stalking is different. It's not about care. It's about power.

Sometimes he would follow me to the store, park where he thought I wouldn't see him, and wait. I'd be loading my groceries and spot his vehicle pulling out to beat me home. Other times, I'd come home to find him parked down the street. Not getting ready for dinner. Not texting. Just… watching. Sitting. Waiting.

I don't know what he was waiting for. Sometimes he'd move a little closer. Sometimes he'd sit there for hours before finally coming home himself. It wasn't love. It wasn't protection. It was intimidation masked as attention.

Stalking doesn't always look like trespassing or tracking apps. Sometimes it looks like a truck parked just far enough away to make you question whether it's really happening—until it keeps happening.

## Gaslighting 101

One night, I found him texting someone in the middle of the night. I asked, calmly, "Who is that?" He laughed. "Just someone wanting to know about something you wouldn't understand."

Then came the silence. The stonewalling. The punishment.

By the next morning, I was apologizing—for asking the question.

That's gaslighting: when you start to believe their version of reality over your own. When you trust their story more than your gut. When you apologize for something they did.

He was texting a new girlfriend who lived in another state. They had a whole sexting thing going on. I confronted it, but the gaslighting had twisted me so much that even when the truth was staring me in the face, I minimized it, questioned myself, and pushed it aside.

## The Rules Keep Changing

At first, it was okay to talk to friends. Then, suddenly, it was a problem. My friends weren't good people or good for me to be around.

At first, I could participate in things at church or with family and friends. Then, my community work was viewed as opportunities for affairs and my time with family and friends were robbing him. And it didn't stop with my time or my relationships. Even my body wasn't mine to protect.

At first, I could say "no" to sex. Then, suddenly, saying no meant I was broken, selfish, or punishing him. Once I had the flu and was returning to bed from vomiting in the toilet. He had the solution to my flu and nausea – a special gift – sex. Really? I was not given "No' as an option. That wasn't intimacy. It wasn't protection. It certainly wasn't a "special gift." It was a violation. And that's how the rules kept shifting—what started as choice became obligation, and what should have been safety became control.

No matter how hard I tried, I kept losing. Because the rules kept changing—and I was never told the new ones. Every day I was walking on eggshells, wondering when the next episode would come.

I was constantly failing a test I didn't know I was taking. Each new rule tightened the rope a little more.

## When "Perfect" Is an Insult

Not all name-calling sounds harsh. Sometimes it hides behind a grin. Sometimes it comes as a "compliment" with venom tucked just beneath the surface. For me, it was the word *perfect*.

"You're so perfect," he'd say—but it wasn't praise. It was a jab. A way to tell me I was too good for him. That I thought I was better. That I was the problem. He used the word like it was an accusation, like being dependable, kind, or clear-minded was a threat.

Being called *perfect* wasn't about admiration. It was about making me feel like I had to shrink. Like I had to apologize for having standards. Like my worth made him feel small—and so I had to pay for it.

Name-calling doesn't always show up in shouting. Sometimes it's subtle. Dismissive. Mocking. But it lands just the same: it tells you that being you is a burden, or not enough, or somehow wrong. And over time, even the smallest word can start to shape your silence.

## The Trap Tightens

He controlled the narrative, the mood of the house. He decided when we talked, what we talked about, and when the talking stopped.

He gave the silent treatment for days—weeks—even months but when *I* got quiet, he'd explode: "Why are you treating me so badly? Do you have a *boyfriend*?"

He'd "joke" in front of others, then comment on my inability to participate in the conversation. He'd tell me he was the only one for me, he owned me—and somehow I believed him. He threatened suicide if I didn't comply. Love-bombing one day. Threats the next. I was trapped on a roller coaster I couldn't get off.

Today, "You are the love of my life." The next day "I wish I'd never married you."

Today, "I will do anything for you." The next day, "I want a divorce."

Today, "I'm a great person. You are lucky to have me. We will build a great life." The next day, "When you get home I won't be here. I took a bunch of pills."

Back and forth, up and down, round and round. Jerking left. Ripping to the right. Blindsiding me over and over. I couldn't find my footing.

## Where the Rules Were Never Fair to Begin With

Emotional abuse doesn't happen in a vacuum—it happens inside systems shaped by culture, gender roles, and race. If you grew up as a woman in a household or faith tradition where silence, submission, or service were expected, your voice may have been stifled long before any relationship. If you're a person of color, you may have been taught not only to endure pain but to carry it with a smile—because the world may not believe you, protect you, or give you room to break.

If that's part of your story, know this: your truth matters. Your pain is valid. You deserved safety—not stereotypes. And you are allowed to heal loudly.

And that healing begins the moment you name what they tried to normalize.

## When Culture Covers the Truth

Sometimes abuse doesn't look like abuse—because culture has dressed it up in more acceptable clothes. You're taught to endure. To forgive. To be the bigger person. To hold it together. Maybe you heard that love is patient, that good women don't give up, that family is forever.

But those same messages can make you question your pain.

If your upbringing taught you that being "good" means staying quiet, serving others, or keeping the peace at all costs, you might have missed the signs of emotional harm. Or maybe you saw them—but believed it was your job to fix it.

Let me be clear:
*What harms you is not holy.*
*What erases you is not love.*
*And what culture normalizes; you are allowed to name as abuse.*

Breaking free isn't just about leaving a person. Sometimes, it's about waking up from a system that taught you to disappear.

## Is This Abuse?

I didn't have bruises. I had confusion. I didn't have broken bones. I had a broken spirit. I didn't have proof. I had stories that no one else believed—except maybe you.

When the world around you tells you to endure, when the people closest to you say things like "every relationship has its ups and downs," you start to wonder if it's really that bad. If maybe you're the problem. If maybe this is just what love requires.

If you're reading this and wondering, *"Is what I'm going through abuse?"* let me gently say: If you're even asking the question—something's not right. Abuse doesn't always look like violence. Sometimes it looks like being constantly blamed, questioned, or dismissed. Sometimes it's silence that punishes. Sometimes it's kindness that comes right after cruelty, just long enough to make you doubt yourself.

Healthy love doesn't leave you confused, afraid to speak, second-guessing your memories, or constantly apologizing for things that aren't your fault.

You're not "too sensitive." You're not imagining it. And you're not alone.

---

### Self-Check: Are You in an Emotionally Abusive Dynamic?

*Emotional abuse can be hard to name—especially when there are no visible bruises. But patterns don't lie. If you recognize yourself in any of these, it's okay to call it what it is.*

- You feel like you're always "messing up," even when you try your best.

- You're afraid to speak up because of how they'll react.
- You're blamed for everything—even their moods.
- You question your memory of events.
- You question your ability to make decisions or even care for yourself.
- You feel disoriented—like your own thoughts and instincts can't be trusted.
- You start to wonder if you're the problem—even when something doesn't feel right.
- You feel threatened or intimidated.
- You are being sexually managed.
- You have been separated from family and friends.
- You are prevented from doing things you want.
- You feel like a possession.
- You are being threatened with violence.
- You are being repeatedly interrogated about where you have been.
- You have to "manage" their emotions constantly.
- You are getting calls or texts making sure you are where you said you would be.
- You feel like you're not allowed to feel anything at all.
- You feel like there's no way out.
- You keep hoping the "good version" of them will come back.

## Ways to Reclaim Yourself

I have a secret I want to tell you right now. No matter what anyone has told you, no matter how anyone has treated you – YOU MATTER!

You don't need to wait for someone else to validate your pain.

You don't need bruises to call it abuse.

You don't need permission to protect yourself.

You are allowed to redefine what safety and peace look like—and to act on that, in your own time and way.

You can turn your negatives into positives.

You can forgive yourself.

You can get help and support from friends, family, and therapists.

Abuse thrives in silence—but healing starts with truth. And here's the truth: You don't deserve to live under someone else's shifting rules.

## Say It. Write It. Own It.

*They made you question everything you thought you knew. You were being manipulated. Now speak the truth that sets you free—because your healing begins the moment you believe yourself.*

## Journal Prompt #1:

*Write about a time when the "rules" in your relationship suddenly shifted. How did you feel? What message did it send you about your safety or worth?*

## Journal Prompt #2:

*Have you ever been told you're "too sensitive," "too emotional," or that "you imagined it"? What do you wish you could say back to that now?*

## Exercise: Reclaim Your Reality

### Step 1: Write Your Truth
- Choose one confusing incident from your past—something you were gaslighted about.
- Without censoring, write down **exactly** how it happened *as you remember it.*
- Then write what the other person told you happened—or how they reacted to your version.

### Step 2: Validate Yourself
- Now ask yourself:
  - What did I see?
  - What did I feel in my body?
  - What would I believe if someone I loved told me this same story?
- Write a validation statement for yourself as if you were a trusted friend.

### Example:
"You were not overreacting. You were hurt. Your feelings made sense. What happened to you was not okay."

# I Know Who I Am

## Step 3: Create a Truth List

- List five things you now know to be true—even if someone else tried to make you doubt them.
    - Ex: "I deserve respect." "I can remember exactly what happened." "Kindness doesn't mean control." "Silence is not safety." "Love shouldn't hurt."

*Gaslighting loses power the moment you stop arguing and start believing yourself again. Your truth is enough.*

*I am being true to myself.*

## Chapter 8

# Why Boundaries Felt Like Betrayal

I remember the first time I tried to set a boundary. It wasn't dramatic—I didn't yell or give an ultimatum. I just said I was going out to breakfast with a friend. But instead of respect, I was met with anger. The silence that followed was colder than any argument, punctuated by a tirade of accusations about the affair I must be having. I had known her since our children were small. He knew her too. Where was this coming from? I started to wonder if I'd done something wrong by asking for what I needed.

Once you realize the rules are designed to control you, you start trying to set boundaries. That's when the real backlash begins.

## Survival Erased My Boundaries

As I look back now, I had solidly moved into survival mode. Every day felt like driving blindfolded—never knowing which mood swing or accusation would send the entire day spiraling. When you are living with someone who is abusive this can be how you feel every day, hour by hour, minute by minute. Because of the constant confusion and unstable environment, we often self-protect by going into survival mode.

# I Know Who I Am

If you are hiking in the mountains and a bear shows up, your adrenaline is going to pump like crazy. Your survival instincts will kick in. I'm sure you've heard or read that there are three basic survival instincts: flight, fight, or freeze. But there's a fourth response that isn't talked about as often—fawn. And for many of us, especially in emotionally abusive relationships, it's the one we learned best.

Fawning means trying to please, pacify, or appease someone to avoid conflict or harm. It can look like over-apologizing, avoiding disagreement, or staying silent even when something hurts—just to keep the peace. I didn't realize that constantly trying to fix his moods, meet his needs, and keep things "calm" wasn't love. It was survival.

One of his obsessions was flying expensive, radio-controlled airplanes. He said it helped his depression, that it made him feel better—happy. So when he used money meant for household bills to buy a new plane, I didn't protest. When he took it out and crashed it, I told him, "Well, you're learning. It'll go better next time. At least you had fun for a while." Then he would buy another. When the bills piled up, I told myself I'd figure it out somehow. Because after every crash, he would lock himself in his room for days, shutting me out and leaving me to carry the weight of holding everything together.

That wasn't love. That was survival.

That was *fawning*.

When your nervous system is stuck in that mode, boundaries feel impossible. Speaking up feels risky. And even though part of you knows it's not right—you're just trying to make it through another day. But the truth is: survival mode isn't meant to be permanent. You're allowed to stop shrinking and start reclaiming your voice.

When the adrenaline starts pumping and your body begins to stress, then the cortisol and other stress hormones start shooting through your body. That's great when the bear is moving closer. It's not so great when you live that way every day just to survive your circumstances.

Too much survival stress is not a good thing. When your body's stuck in survival mode, the idea of setting boundaries doesn't feel brave—it feels dangerous. And when you've been fawning for so long, it can feel selfish to say no. But it's not. It's necessary. And you're allowed to learn how to set boundaries.

## When My Body Became the Target

He liked it when I looked a certain way—when I spent time on my hair, when I wore something he felt showed me off. I was supposed to be his accessory. A reflection of his taste. Something polished. Something praised.

But I didn't like being on display. It felt like I was being presented, not seen. So eventually, I stopped. I stopped dressing for attention. I stopped bending myself into someone else's fantasy. I started trying to be comfortable in my own skin again.

That's when the attention ceased.

When I wasn't perfectly put together, he barely noticed me. When I wasn't performing beauty, I wasn't worth his gaze. I could be working, cooking, showing up in every way that mattered—and still be invisible. Unless I looked really, really good, I didn't exist to him.

And then came the weight. I ate healthy. I exercised. But the stress lived in my body. The anxiety, the walking-on-eggshells days, the effort of trying to survive—that doesn't just go away. My body did what it had to do: it protected me. It softened, it held, it stored. And as I gained weight, I stopped being a showpiece.

He stopped touching me. Most of the time, he wouldn't even be in the same room.

That wasn't love. That was performance-based acceptance. That was body shaming dressed up as standards.

This body, the one he ignored and criticized, was the same body that kept me alive. It carried the weight of everything I couldn't speak. It stayed and endured. It whispered truth when I tried to forget it.

And now? I refuse to apologize for the shape I became while surviving. It protected me when nothing else could. I don't owe anyone beauty or performance. What I owe is this:

Kindness to the body that stayed.

Gratitude for the strength it held.

Compassion for the parts of me that carried it all.

My body deserves tenderness and safety. It deserves to be loved—not for how it looks, but for what it's lived through.

## When You Push Back, They Push Harder

The first time I set a real boundary, it felt like I was asking permission to breathe. I wasn't yelling. I wasn't even angry. I just said, "That doesn't work for me."

He looked at me like I'd just betrayed him. The air changed. My stomach dropped. I felt like I'd broken some sacred rule. But I hadn't—I'd just spoken a boundary.

I remember once, he made last-minute plans to have someone come over to discuss a business proposition. I had just gotten home from work—exhausted, overwhelmed, and already behind on a dozen things. I said gently, "Tonight doesn't work for me. I need rest. You all can talk, but I'll just be upstairs."

His face hardened. He didn't yell at first. He didn't need to. The shift in energy was enough to fill the room with tension. Minutes later, the silent treatment began. Then came the accusations—selfish, inconsiderate, impossible to please. He said I must not want this person to come over because I was having an affair—with someone I'd never even met.

He told me I was ruining everything.

What I expected was a conversation. What I got was an explosion.

And that's when I began to realize: boundaries don't break healthy relationships—they reveal unhealthy ones.

## Abusers Don't Like Losing Control

Boundaries aren't offensive. They're healthy. But when someone's whole power comes from controlling you, your boundary feels like a threat.

Suddenly, I wasn't the "sweet, supportive" partner anymore—I was "selfish," "cold," and "disrespectful."

He told me I was cruel for saying no. He said I was abandoning him. That I was heartless. And for a while, I believed him. Once guilt takes the wheel, your truth gets shoved in the trunk.

## Guilt is a Weapon

Guilt-tripping didn't always sound angry. Sometimes it came as hundreds of texts—begging me to just call him back. Then, when I didn't respond immediately, the tone would shift:

*"I guess you don't care."*
*"You're just like everyone else."*
*"I hope you're happy ignoring someone who loves you."*

Other times, it came as a wounded silence, followed by a flood of "poor me" messages designed to make me feel like the villain. If I didn't respond quickly, the tone would shift—accusations would replace pleading. Somehow, I always ended up feeling like I had done something wrong, just for needing space or asking for something different. That's the trap of guilt-tripping: it turns your self-respect into something you have to defend.

The pressure wasn't just to answer the phone. It was to fix his feelings. To soothe his ego. To carry the weight of his loneliness so he didn't have to.

Guilt-tripping is a form of emotional manipulation—it makes you feel responsible for someone else's mood, their pain, even their choices. And when that burden gets heavy enough, you start losing sight of your own voice underneath it.

I was told I had "changed." That I "used to be so easy to be around." That I was "too perfect." The message was the same: whatever I was in that moment, it wasn't acceptable. The rules kept shifting, and no matter what I did, I was always wrong.

## When Growth Looks Like Betrayal

And the truth? I *had* changed. I was waking up. I was saying no. I was drawing lines in the sand.

But in a toxic relationship, growth feels like betrayal—because your growth threatens their grip.

## The Drama Dial Turns Up

The more I tried to detach, the more chaotic things became—fights over nothing, icy silences that lasted for days, and accusations that made no sense. It wasn't resolution he wanted—it was re-entry. Control. Compliance.

Suddenly, everything was always urgent, always dramatic, always my fault.

Once, I said I needed time to finish something I was working on. Suddenly, it became proof that I didn't care enough about him. He disappeared for hours and returned early the next morning, accusing me of wanting someone else. I spent days reassuring him, even though I was the one who needed comfort.

I started walking on eggshells *again*—but now I was angry about it.

## Why Backlash Hurts So Much

Here's what makes backlash so confusing: when you finally start doing healthy things—speaking up, asking for space, telling the truth—you get punished for it.

So I stopped asserting myself. I called it 'keeping the peace,' but the truth was—I didn't believe I deserved peace unless it came without a fight.

The backlash to my boundaries sent a damaging message: "Your health is harmful." And if you're not grounded in your worth yet, you might internalize it.

That's how abuse becomes self-sustaining. Every attempt to escape is met with pain—so you stop trying.

> **Self-check: Are You Facing Backlash for Setting Boundaries?**
>
> If setting boundaries feels like danger instead of safety, you might be facing emotional backlash. Here's are some ways to recognize it:
>
> - Do they accuse you of being selfish when you speak up?
> - Do they escalate emotionally when you calmly say "no"?
> - Do they act disappointed in your choices?
> - Do they act critical of your choices?
> - Do you feel scared or ashamed after asserting yourself?
> - Do they throw false accusations at you?
> - Do they punish you with silence, rage, or guilt?
> - Do you feel like "peace" only happens when you give in?
>
> If yes—you're not overreacting. You're experiencing manipulation.

## Ways to Reclaim Yourself

The backlash isn't proof that you're wrong—it's proof that you're growing. Here's what helped me:

- I stopped justifying my boundaries. I started holding them quietly.
- I removed my autopilot. I started making quality decisions – big and small.
- I stopped being in reactive mode.
- I started doing better self-care. I ate better and got good sleep.
- I no longer accepted blame that wasn't mine but embraced understanding instead.
- I reminded myself: **I am not responsible for his reaction.**
- I had a support system I could check in with—a friend, a therapist, someone safe.
- I wrote down what happened so I wouldn't rewrite history.
- I gave myself permission to grieve—boundaries bring freedom, but also loss.
- I forgave myself.
- I chose to live in the present not the past or the hope of a false future.
- I took responsibility for myself.
- I reclaimed my personal rights and power.
- I started responding instead of reacting.
- I forgave him. That doesn't mean I was ok with being treated like he treated me. It meant I stopped waiting for closure from him—and gave it to myself. Forgiveness wasn't about excusing him. It was about releasing me..

Eventually, I learned this: **Healthy people respect limits. Abusive people test them.**

And I was finally done being tested.

## Say It. Write It. Own It.

*Setting boundaries can feel like betrayal when you've been trained to abandon yourself. But every time you choose your truth over their comfort, you're reclaiming your power.*

## Journal Prompt #1:

*What were you taught—explicitly or implicitly—about saying no? What were the consequences (real or feared) when you tried to assert your needs?*

## Journal Prompt #2:

*Think about a time when someone reacted badly to one of your boundaries. What did you learn about them in that moment? What did you learn about yourself?*

## Exercise: Begin Building Boundaries

### Step 1: Identify Your Leaks
- Write down three areas where your boundaries were (or are) frequently crossed. Examples:
    - "I felt guilty saying no to things I didn't want to do."
    - "I stayed in conversations that made me feel unsafe."
    - "I explained myself when I didn't need to."

### Step 2: Write Your Boundary Wish List
- For each time your boundary was crossed, write the boundary you wish you could have voiced.
    - "I'm not available for that."
    - "Please don't raise your voice at me."
    - "I'm not discussing this any further."
    - "No is a full sentence."

### Step 3: Set One Silent Boundary
- Choose one boundary from your list that you can begin enforcing **without saying a word**.
    - It could be leaving a room.
    - Not replying to a guilt-tripping text.
    - Logging off.
    - Taking longer to respond.
- Then write about how it felt. Was it hard? Was it freeing?

---

*Boundaries are not confrontations. They are conversations with yourself about what you will and will not allow. You are allowed to take up space—and to protect it.*

*I am peaceful and calm.*

## CHAPTER 9

# Healing in the Eye of the Storm

I used to think healing would begin after everything calmed down—after I figured it all out. But it didn't wait. I remember sitting in the park, watching the water roll by, listening to the birds, just breathing. I wasn't crying. I wasn't spiraling. I was just... still. And in that stillness, something inside me whispered, You don't have to live like this forever. It didn't feel like healing at the time. But it was the first crack of light.

Healing doesn't wait until it's safe. Sometimes it starts in the middle of the chaos—quietly, stubbornly, like a seed pushing through concrete.

## Healing Doesn't Have to Wait

People assume healing starts after something ends. But mine started while I was still deep in the storm. It began in secret. Quiet. Barely visible from the outside. I was reading books about it. I started seeing a therapist—just during lunch breaks, quietly, so no one would know. Then something shifted—I stopped asking, *"How can I make this work?"* and started asking, *"What's happening to me?"*

That's when I started choosing me.

## Tiny Acts of Self-Return

I didn't throw down ultimatums or make grand speeches. I just started doing small, defiant things that reminded me I existed.

- I ordered what *I* wanted at restaurants.
- I wore lipstick again.
- I read books that made me feel strong.
- I became more involved at church.
- I went through a program of healing & recovery.
- I went for walks without asking.
- I started taking classes again.
- I stopped wearing only black and pink and got colors I liked and felt comfortable in.
- I journaled so much I ended up turning my words into a book
- I stopped explaining myself.

These weren't acts of rebellion—they were acts of remembering.

## Healing Begins With Permission

I gave myself permission to feel things I'd buried:

- **Anger** – not the explosive kind, but the kind that says, *"I didn't deserve that."*
- **Sadness** – the slow, silent ache for the life I thought I was building.
- **Confusion** – the kind that clouds everything and makes you question your sanity.
- **Grief** – for the version of me that stayed quiet too long.
- **Loneliness** – even when he was right there beside me.
- **Disgust** – not just at him, but at how much of myself I had lost.
- **Numbness** – the scariest of all, because it felt like nothing could reach me.

- **Hope** – fragile at first, but real. A tiny light that whispered, *You're still in there.*

I let myself want more—even if I didn't know how to get it yet. I let myself mourn the fantasy of who I thought he was. And most importantly: I stopped pretending this was love.

## You Don't Need to Be "Fully Healed" to Grow

Peace doesn't wait until everything is resolved. It begins in the small, quiet moments where you choose yourself—tenderly, imperfectly, consistently. Fear doesn't disappear overnight, but courage can still show up in its presence. A strong choice doesn't require the absence of fear—just the presence of truth.

Closure isn't something another person grants you. Sometimes it begins the moment you stop waiting for their apology and start offering yourself compassion instead.

Healing isn't a destination you reach—it's a direction you walk in. One step at a time. One truth at a time. One brave breath after another.

## When the Pain Isn't Just Yours

I wasn't the only one who lived in that house. And I wasn't the only one affected by what happened inside it.

Abuse doesn't stay contained—it seeps into the walls, into the air, into the spaces where children are trying to grow up. Even if they aren't the direct target, they absorb the tension. They feel the fear. They learn to walk on eggshells. To quiet their voices. To read the room like their safety depends on it—because sometimes, it does.

Sometimes, the grief isn't just for what I endured. It's for what they saw. For what they felt but didn't know how to name. For the moments I couldn't protect them because I was still learning how to protect myself.

Even if your children aren't the direct target, they feel it. They learn to shrink themselves to avoid the next explosion. They hide in their rooms, stop inviting friends over, stop reaching for connection. They grow up too fast—or shut down altogether.

I saw it in mine.

They became emotionally distant. One stopped wanting hugs. Another poured themselves into perfectionism or rebellion—anything to regain a sense of control. They didn't always have the words, but their bodies told the truth. They were anxious. On edge. Hyper-independent. And I didn't always know how to reach them, because I was still learning how to reach myself.

And that's what breaks your heart as a parent. You know they're hurting—but you're trying to survive, too.

The grief isn't just for what I endured. It's for what they carried without ever being handed the tools to understand it.

I didn't choose the abuse. But I get to choose healing. And when I began healing, something shifted in them, too. Maybe not overnight. But eventually, they saw something different: a mother who was learning to protect peace, speak the truth, and offer herself the love she never received.

Healing doesn't just free you. It changes the atmosphere for everyone who's been holding their breath beside you.

Before you move on, take a moment to check in with yourself. Healing isn't just about what changes around you—it's about what's shifting inside you. And when you begin to care for your own pain, you start changing the atmosphere around you, too.

## Self-Check: Are You Starting to Choose You?

*Even in survival mode, small shifts matter. Healing often begins with subtle acts of self-loyalty—the quiet moments when you stop abandoning yourself. These signs might seem small, but they're powerful indicators that something inside you is waking up.*

- Do you notice when something feels wrong—even if you stay silent?
- Are you less interested in their opinion and more in your own?
- Are you beginning to set boundaries?
- Have you stopped trying to "earn" love?
- Do you have moments of clarity you used to ignore?
- Are you educating yourself about abuse?
- Are you beginning to give yourself small moments of care—like rest, nourishment, or quiet time just for you?
- Are you beginning to imagine a life beyond this?
- Have you started building your tribe, so you have a strong support system?
- Have you started thinking about a safety plan?
- Have you asked for help?
- Have you started looking at your future?

If so—you're already healing.

## Ways to Reclaim Yourself

Here's what I did that helped me start choosing myself—even while I was still in it:

- **I journaled** like I was writing to the version of me who would one day be free. Sometimes I wrote letters to her. Sometimes I wrote letters *from* her.
- **I moved my body**—not to change how I looked, but to remember I had one. Walks, stretches, dancing in the kitchen. Just enough to say, *"I'm still here."*
- **I asked myself,** *"What would I do if I weren't afraid?"* And sometimes I did the thing anyway—even if I was shaking.
- **I stopped apologizing** for being tired, sensitive, emotional, overwhelmed, angry, or human.
- **I made space for joy** in small doses: music I loved, shows that made me laugh, food that tasted like comfort.
- **I built boundaries** that didn't need to be announced. I just quietly stopped explaining myself.
- **I stopped explaining my pain** to people committed to misunderstanding it.
- **I found community**—books, blogs, support groups, podcasts, and people who had walked this same fire and made it out alive.
- **I stopped asking for permission** to heal, feel, or live in truth. I gave it to myself.
- **I spoke truth into mirrors**—out loud. "You don't deserve this." "You are allowed to want peace." "You are still worth loving."
- **I celebrated the quiet, hard-won victories:** Saying no. Not reacting. Sleeping through the night. Remembering what I liked. Smiling at myself, even just once.

Each small act was a crack in the armor of the life I had built to survive. And through those cracks, light started coming in. You don't have to leave to begin healing. You only have to decide: **I choose me.**

## Say It. Write It. Own It.

*You don't have to wait for everything to change before you start healing. It begins the moment you believe your story matters—and choose, even quietly, to come back to yourself. Every time you choose you, that's power.*

## Journal Prompt #1:

*What small act of self-respect or defiance have you done recently—even if no one else noticed? How did it feel in your body, mind, or spirit?*

## Journal Prompt #2:

*What does "choosing yourself" mean to you today? How is it different from how you were taught to show up in relationships?*

## Exercise: Your Quiet Rebellion

### Step 1: Spot the Shift

Write about the moment you first started to feel differently. It could be the moment you stopped reacting to him, started imagining life without him, or said "no" in your head, even if not out loud.

- What changed?
- What did you notice in yourself?
- Did it scare or excite you?

**Step 2: Make a Micro Choice for You**
Pick one tiny act of healing you can do today—and then do it.
Examples:
- Wear something you feel good in—even if it's not what they'd approve of.
- Text someone who makes you laugh.
- Journal in a place that feels like yours.
- Sit in silence and just breathe.

**Step 3: Write Yourself a Promise**
Finish this sentence:
"Right here, right now, but I promise myself…"
Write 3-5 lines to affirm your healing, even inside the storm.

*Healing begins the moment you choose yourself—even if t he storm around you hasn't calmed.*

*I am healing —one step at a time.*

## Chapter 10

# The Thing That Kept Me Alive Was Killing Me

I remember bending over backward to fix something that wasn't mine to fix—again. He was angry about something he thought I did but I didn't do, and I still found myself offering solutions, smoothing things over, making dinner, making it easier, making myself smaller. Later that night, I looked in the mirror and thought, Who am I trying to save—and why do I keep losing myself in the process?

The survival tools that helped you cope—numbing, fixing, pleasing, hiding—don't just vanish. They cling. Even when they start to cost you everything.

### This Kept Me Alive (But It's Killing Me)

I didn't set out to numb myself. I didn't consciously decide to disappear beneath food, noise, work, busyness, playing games on my phone, perfection, people-pleasing. I was just trying to breathe. The truth was too loud. The silence was too sharp. The pain was too close.

So I did what I had to do:

I quieted it.
I blurred the edges.
I survived.

## Coping Isn't Weakness. It's Strategy.

Coping is what you do when **you don't have what you need, and you can't get out.** It's not a flaw in your character—it's a response to pain, powerlessness, and emotional overload.

You don't cope because you're broken. You cope because your nervous system said, *"We can't handle this all at once."* So, it did what it had to: it reduced the volume so you could keep functioning. You did what your nervous system knew to do. That's wisdom, not weakness.

Maybe your coping looked like:

- Keeping busy so you didn't have to feel.
- Drinking just enough to fall asleep without thinking.
- Saying "yes" so no one would be mad.
- Keeping the house perfect so it looked like *you* were the problem, not the relationship.
- Taking care of everyone else so you don't have to look at your own loneliness.
- Checking out in front of a screen because silence felt too loud.
- Shutting down instead of speaking up—because speaking never made anything better.

**Whatever your strategy was, it had a logic.** It gave you a sense of control when the rest of your life felt like chaos.

The world might have praised your coping:

- "You're so strong."
- "You're always so put together."
- "You're amazing under pressure."

But no one saw that your strength was your shield. That your calm was your collapse. That your competence was your cry for help.

You weren't thriving. You were surviving. And survival deserves compassion—not shame.

## But Then the Coping Started to Cost You Something

At first, it helped. It dulled the ache. It made the days manageable. But overtime, it took something too:

- Your joy
- Your presence
- Your ability to hear yourself think
- Your access to real connection
- Your softness
- Your truth

It became its own trap. And slowly, the thing that helped you survive started keeping you from living.

## What You Called Control Was Just Containment

You weren't really in control. You were containing the chaos. You micromanaged everything so you didn't fall apart. You performed competence while internally unraveling. You made everything look fine so no one would ask questions. And maybe no one did.

But that doesn't mean you were okay.

There were mornings driving to work when the radio was turned up so loud the windows rattled—not out of joy, but desperation. Anything to drown out the thoughts. To silence the replay of the last outburst. To keep the pain at bay. Crying wasn't an option. Feeling wasn't safe. The noise was a shield. The beat, a distraction. Some days, survival meant disappearing into sound—just to make it through the day.

## Coping Helped You Not Feel. Healing Helps You Feel Safely

Coping says: *"You're not allowed to feel this. It's too much."* Healing says: *"You can feel this now—and you won't be destroyed by it."*

When you were in survival mode, your emotions had to stay small or silent. You couldn't fall apart. You couldn't scream. You couldn't cry for too long. You had to keep going. Keep fixing. Keep smiling. Keep appearing strong.

So, your feelings got stuffed down—buried under responsibility, control, numbness, or performance.

But healing teaches you this:

- A wave of grief doesn't mean you're broken.
- A spike of anger doesn't mean you're unsafe.
- A tender ache doesn't mean you've gone backward.

It means your mind, body and spirit are finally *processing* what they didn't have time or space to feel before.

## You start learning that emotions aren't enemies.

They're messengers.

- Anxiety might mean: *"You need space."*
- Sadness might mean: *"You're grieving something real."*
- Anger might mean: *"You've been crossed."*
- Numbness might mean: *"You're at your limit."*
- Guilt might mean: *"You've been conditioned to believe your needs are wrong."*
- Shame might mean: *"Someone taught you that your pain makes you unworthy."*
- Fear might mean: *"Your body remembers something your mind tried to forget."*

- Confusion might mean: *"You're waking up from a story that never honored your truth."*

You begin to listen to what your body is trying to say—without judging it or silencing it. And over time, what used to feel like emotional chaos becomes information.

These feelings aren't the problem. They're the invitation—to tend to yourself instead of abandoning yourself.

Just because someone else survived differently doesn't mean the way you survived was wrong.

## You Don't Need to Shame the Way You Survived

You get to say: *"That kept me alive."*

And also: *"I don't want to live like that anymore."*

You don't have to justify why you coped the way you did. You only have to decide what you need now. You don't need to be perfect. You just need to stop leaving yourself behind.

Coping helped you survive. But healing lets you choose something better. And you're allowed to outgrow what once protected you.

Then I realized:

The thing that kept me alive was also the thing that kept me stuck.

Survival helped me make it through. But it couldn't take me any further.

I didn't need to hustle for love.

I needed to learn how to care for myself.

## What Self-Care Really Looks Like

Self-care isn't just bubble baths and breathing exercises. It's not about escaping your life—it's about tending to it. Caring for yourself can be quiet, fierce, tender, or bold. It can be emotional, spiritual, physical, or practical.

Sometimes self-care is:

- Turning off your phone for an hour so your mind can breathe.
- Eating something nourishing—even if no one sees it.
- Saying no to a call or visit because you need rest.
- Crying in the shower without rushing to "get it together."
- Scheduling a therapy appointment—or showing up for one.
- Letting someone help you without apologizing for needing it.
- Drinking water. Going outside. Stretching your body.
- Speaking to yourself with kindness—even when it feels awkward.
- Creating beauty in your space—light a candle, open a window, play music.
- Giving yourself permission to feel joy again, without guilt.
- Stepping away from media and enjoying the quiet.
- Eating when you're hungry. Resting when you're tired.
- Making a space that's just yours—a quiet corner, a playlist, a ritual.
- Asking someone for help. That's not weakness—it's wisdom.
- Writing in a journal to hear your own voice again.
- Taking a walk, visiting a park, or photographing flowers—let the breeze meet your face.
- Trying something new—like a class that interests you.
- Painting, sketching, or coloring just because it feels good.
- Watching a favorite movie that brings comfort or joy.
- Planting something and watching it grow.
- Writing a letter—even if you never send it.
- Watching the sunset and letting yourself exhale.
- Eating a cookie—without guilt, without explanation.

Self-care doesn't have to be expensive, elaborate, or perfectly planned. It just has to be real. It's how you remind yourself: *I matter, too.*

## Self-Check: Are You Still Coping, or Are You Starting to Heal?

Survival trained you to numb, avoid, and perform. Healing invites you to notice, feel, and care. The shift is subtle—but it's real. Here are signs you may be outgrowing survival and beginning to reclaim your life.

- You call yourself "strong," but it often means "emotionally unavailable."
- You get numb when you're overwhelmed, instead of asking what you need.
- You feel anxious when things are calm—like something must be wrong.
- You stay busy so you don't have to sit with what you feel.
- You over function in crisis but collapse when you're alone.
- You say yes to things that drain you—because saying no feels dangerous.
- You depend on routines, substances, or screens to regulate your emotions.
- You fear falling apart, because you're not sure you'd come back from it.
- You feel most in control when you're emotionally distant—even from yourself.
- You can name what everyone else needs—but not what *you* need.

You don't need to feel bad about how you coped. But you get to decide whether you want to keep living that way.

## Ways to Reclaim Yourself

You don't have to rip away every coping mechanism. You just have to stop pretending they're helping you when they're hurting you.

These days, I still sit in the car before work. Not to numb out—but to check in. I ask, "How are you, really?" And I wait for the honest answer.

That's what reclaiming yourself can look like—small, quiet, consistent acts of care.

- Name the behavior you use most when you feel unsafe, overwhelmed, or alone.
  Say it clearly: *"When I feel ___, I usually ___."*
  You can't change what you won't name.

- Write down what that behavior *gives you*—and what it *costs you*.
  Is it peace? Control? Numbness? Distraction?
  What's the price you pay to keep it going?

- Try doing nothing when the urge to numb hits.
  Even for 30 seconds. Let the feeling arrive without chasing it away.
  Ask: *What is this feeling trying to tell me?*

- Choose one way to tend to your nervous system instead of shutting it down.
  Movement, stillness, breath, journaling, water, music, rest.
  Not to fix anything—just to *be with yourself.*

- Say this aloud (or write it down):
  *"I survived in the best ways I knew how.
  But now I'm learning to care for myself, not just escape myself."*

You don't need to be hard on yourself to be honest with yourself. You just need to stop living like you're still in danger.

## Say It. Write It. Own It.

*The most powerful truth you can tell is the one you once silenced. Now's your chance to say it out loud.*

## Journal Prompt #1:

*What's one coping behavior you've depended on to get through pain? What did it help you avoid? What did it protect you from?*

## Journal Prompt #2:

*What would it feel like to meet that same pain with care instead of avoidance? What would care look like for you now?*

## Exercise: Write a Letter to the Behavior That Protected You

**Step 1: Choose the coping mechanism you relied on most.**
Give it a name if it helps—"Perfection," "Numbness," "Overworking," "The Bottle," "Scrolling," "Saying Yes."

**Step 2: Write a short letter to that behavior.**
Start with: *"You showed up when I needed something. Here's what you gave me. Here's what I didn't see. And here's what I'm choosing now."*
Let it be honest. Let it be kind. Let it be yours.

**Step 3: End with this declaration:**
*"I honor the version of me who needed to survive.
But I choose to live now—with presence, not performance."*

*You didn't fail for coping.
You succeeded at staying alive.
And now, you get to learn what
it feels like to stay awake.*

*I am choosing to live, not just survive.*

## CHAPTER 11

# The Moment I Couldn't Pretend Anymore

It wasn't a blowup. It wasn't a crisis. I was just sitting on the porch swing, unable to move. Everything was quiet—a soft breeze blowing. He was upstairs, the dogs were asleep beside me, and I felt like I had nothing left in me—not anger, not sadness, just this bone-deep exhaustion. I wasn't even trying to figure things out anymore. I just knew. I can't do this. Not like this. Not anymore.

Sometimes the truth doesn't land like lightning. It lands like exhaustion. And then, one quiet moment… you finally know: you can't keep living like this.

**The Moment I Knew**

There wasn't a big explosion. No dramatic fight. No visible bruise. No shouting match that changed everything. It was quieter than that.

It was the way he looked at me—like I was the problem for being hurt. It was the moment I realized I was explaining myself again, and I didn't even believe what I was saying. It was the silence in my chest after another apology I didn't owe. It was the moment something inside me whispered, "This can't be love."

It was a slow awakening. There had been many, many single moments. I just hadn't put them together. I just knew I felt rotten most of the time. One day a coworker came to me to share her story and needed a listening ear. When she asked me what I thought about her situation, I told her. "You are right. This person in your life is abusive. I felt everything you said." Then I realized what I said. I did feel everything she said—because I lived it. I froze for a second after the words left my mouth. My stomach flipped. Did I really just admit that out loud? Immediately I wanted to grab it out of the air and tuck it away. I was a pro at minimizing things. I started to open my mouth to say, "It's not so bad." But I didn't. I just let the truth sit there. And for once I didn't try to hide it.

## I Didn't Act on It Right Away

That's the part no one tells you. Knowing doesn't mean leaving. Knowing doesn't mean you're ready to speak. Knowing doesn't mean you're strong enough yet. Sometimes, you know—and you stay. You tell yourself it was a bad day. You focus on the good parts. You keep the peace.

But once you know, you can't un-know. The lie starts to rot. And eventually, even you can't pretend anymore.

## The Knowing Lived in My Body Before I Had Words

It showed up in tension. In headaches. My shoulders scrunched up to my ears tightly. There was nausea after a "conversation" that wasn't a conversation at all. It showed up in the way I paused before speaking. In how I triple-checked my tone. In the shrinking I did without even realizing it.

My body knew.
My heart knew.

## My Heart Knew Before I Could Say It

My heart knew I wasn't safe—not because he hit me, but because I couldn't rest around him. It knew I wasn't loved—not the way I needed to be. Not the way I deserved. It knew the silence wasn't peace—it was punishment. It knew the praise was performance. The apologies were strategies. The kindness was currency.

My heart noticed the things I kept forgiving…and started to wonder why I always had to. It began to ache not just because I was hurting—but because I was *abandoning myself* to keep the illusion alive.

My heart wasn't broken by what he did. It was broken by how long I stayed quiet about it.

And the moment I knew? Was the moment I felt the ache and didn't run from it. I didn't defend it. I didn't reframe it. I just… let it be true.

That ache? That was my heart trying to bring me home. But I wasn't ready to admit it out loud.

## That Moment Was the Beginning of the End

It wasn't the moment everything changed on the outside— it was the moment something shifted inside me. It wasn't the moment I told anyone. But it was the moment the truth started to grow louder than the noise. It was a crack in the denial. A fracture in the story I'd worked so hard to hold together. A shift in my internal loyalty—from them to me.

It was the first time I didn't defend the pain. And that made space for something else: self-respect.

### Self-Check: Did You Already Know?

You may not have said it out loud. But your body, your voice, your heart—something started whispering the truth before you were ready to face it.

- You stopped defending the relationship in your head, even if you still did it out loud.
- You couldn't make excuses for them without feeling hollow.
- You noticed the way you held your breath when they walked in the room.
- You replayed conversations, not to remember what was said—but to justify what was done.
- You started to fantasize about being alone—not because you wanted to be single, but because you wanted to be free.
- You caught yourself thinking, *"If a friend told me this story, I'd tell her to run."*
- You felt the shift in your own voice: less joy, less laughter, less you.
- You imagined telling the truth—and immediately felt afraid of what would happen if you did.
- You caught yourself flinching—not from fear of violence, but from fear of being made small.
- You heard your own voice change around them—quieter, cautious, calculated.
- You dreaded the sound of their car in the driveway.
- You realized you stopped sharing good news because you didn't want it twisted or dismissed.

## The Moment I Couldn't Pretend Anymore

- You laughed at things that hurt—just to keep the peace.
- You started fantasizing about escape, not romance.
- You found yourself clenching your jaw, tensing your shoulders, or holding your breath without noticing.

You knew. Maybe not all at once. Maybe not in words. But you knew.

## Ways to Reclaim Yourself

You don't need a dramatic moment to trust yourself. You don't need a crisis. You don't need proof. You just need to stop walking away from what you already know.

- Write about *the moment you knew*—even if it felt small, strange, or incomplete.
  Start with: "I didn't say anything, but something changed when…"
- Describe what shifted in your body. Where did the knowing live—in your stomach? Your chest? Your silence?
- List the reasons you didn't act on it right away.
  Name them without shame. They protected you when you weren't ready.
- Say this to yourself:
  *"I didn't fail for not acting sooner. I honored what I could when I could."*
- Choose one way to honor your knowing today:
  Speak your truth to a safe person. Write a letter you don't send. Set one boundary that says, *"I don't need to wait for it to get worse."*

You don't have to wait for everything to fall apart to stop betraying yourself.

## Say It. Write It. Own It.

*You knew before you could say it—and now, it's time to honor that knowing out loud.*

## Journal Prompt #1:

*What was the moment you knew something wasn't right—before you could admit it out loud? Write it like a memory, not a confession.*

## Journal Prompt #2:

*What did you tell yourself to stay? What would you say to that version of yourself now?*

## Exercise: Write to the One Who Knew

**Step 1: Write a letter to the version of yourself who knew but stayed.**
You can begin with:
*"You saw it. You felt it. And I forgive you for not being ready."*
Don't shame her. Don't fix her. Just meet her with truth and compassion.

## The Moment I Couldn't Pretend Anymore

**Step 2: Read the letter back and underline one sentence that feels like a turning point.**
Let it live in your journal or copy it onto a sticky note.
Keep it close when doubt tries to rewrite your memory.

**Step 3: Say this aloud:**
*"I didn't imagine it. I didn't overreact.
I knew—and now, I'm listening."*

*Your knowing was not the end.
It was the beginning of
your return to yourself.*

*I am becoming
the person
I choose to be.*

## Chapter 12

# The Truth Hurt, But So Did the Lie

I had finally admitted the truth out loud—to myself, and then to a friend. I didn't try to soften it or explain it away. I just said it: "This is abusive." And immediately, I wished I could take it back. I felt like I'd betrayed him... like I'd betrayed us. But it was the truth. And once I named it, everything I'd buried came rushing in—the gaslighting, the blame, the silence, the fear. It felt like my heart cracked open all at once.

Knowing doesn't mean it stops hurting. In fact, the moment the truth lands—really lands—it can break your heart. But lying to yourself breaks you slowly, and for much longer.

### My Excuses Were Just Dressed Up Lies

Some of you may be asking, "Why did you put up with this behavior?" That is a very good question. I think there were a few reasons. Looking back, I know I was deep in avoidance—coping, yes, but also in denial that I was being abused. If I avoided what was really happening and covered it with excuses that seemed somewhat valid, then I could keep moving forward.

But excuses are just lies we convince ourselves are truths to avoid a painful situation or something we don't want to do.

I remember holidays and birthdays—they were always especially hard. I'd spend hours cooking a big meal for the whole family, trying to create something joyful. He would make something separate for himself, then lock himself in the bedroom and refuse to come down. Guests would arrive, and I'd be smiling and serving food, pretending everything was fine—while the silence upstairs spoke volumes. Sometimes he got a hotel room and stayed there until everyone left. I told myself he was socially shy. That he needed space. That he'd come around eventually. But deep down, I was already grieving something I hadn't admitted was broken.

I became incredibly good at making those excuses. I'd say things like, "He must not have taken his medicine," or "This is just his illness—he doesn't mean to hurt me." He did have diagnoses, and medications stacked high, but none of that erased the damage. I used it as another excuse to minimize the truth. I even told myself he was just tired, grasping for any explanation that made the pain make sense. The truth was, I needed those excuses. They helped me survive what I wasn't ready to name.

But the truth has a way of creeping in—like sunlight under a door. You can pretend it's not there. You can draw the curtains, turn off the lights, focus on anything else. But once it slips in, even in slivers, you start to see what you were never meant to ignore.

I kept trying to live in the dark because it felt safer. But deep down, I was aching for the light.

I didn't want to see it. I told myself I couldn't handle it. But somewhere inside, I think I knew—once the truth found its way in, I wouldn't be able to keep pretending. And maybe that's what scared me most. Not the truth itself… but what I'd have to do once I faced it.

## Denial Is a Survival Tool—Until It Isn't

For a long time, I didn't want to name what was happening. Calling it abuse felt too extreme. Saying I was being controlled felt dramatic. Admitting I was afraid felt like failure. So, I softened it:

"He's just struggling."
"We both have issues."
"I'm probably overreacting."

I told myself it would get better. That love meant staying. That loyalty meant silence.

But here's the truth: It wasn't getting better. It was just getting harder to pretend.

I had a great excuse for every situation. I tried to always make sure there was a sliver of truth in each one, just enough to convince myself. But denial, like dim lighting, can only hide so much. Eventually, the edges start to sharpen. The colors come back into view. And the pain you worked so hard to blur becomes impossible to miss.

We all avoid things. That's just part of life. We avoid people we don't want to talk to. We avoid places we don't want to go, traffic, snake bites, and bee stings. Avoidance isn't inherently wrong. It can be protective. However, when avoiding becomes your normal—when it becomes a lifestyle—it turns into self-abandonment. That's when it stops helping and starts costing you. It keeps you from growing. It dims your joy. It disconnects you from yourself.

Denying an issue exists is a problem. Then there is the constant hope that things would get better. There were those brief moments when he seemed like a great person with great potential. They were so fleeting they were barely recognizable, but I grabbed them and hung on for dear life.

## When Hope Becomes a Trap

Hope can be healing. But in abusive dynamics, hope can become a trap. You hope they'll change. You hope the good days mean something. You hope your love will reach them. You hope they'll wake up one day and realize what they're doing.

But deep down… you know. You know the cycle. You know the apology won't last. You know the next blowup is coming. You know you're breaking.

It's like walking down a path and seeing a snake coil as if to strike. You jump back—that's a natural, life-saving response. In abuse, the same thing happens: you jump back, not always physically, but emotionally, mentally, spiritually. Retreat becomes survival.

But retreat also has a cost. I stopped growing as a person—or at least slowed down. We're meant to keep developing, gaining wisdom, trying new things, creating, evolving. When retreat replaces growth, hope itself shrinks. Life narrows. It becomes about surviving the next strike instead of living fully. I found myself retreating into denial, hoping the pain would disappear if I made myself smaller.

## The Moment It Clicks

There wasn't one big event that changed everything—it was a slow click, like puzzle pieces falling into place. I was watching a movie. A woman on screen said, "This isn't love. This is survival." And I sat there. Frozen. That was me. I wasn't living—I was surviving.

I realized I had spent years managing someone else's feelings, hiding my own, and calling it love. It wasn't love. It was fear, control, obligation, and exhaustion. And I was done pretending it was something else.

## Why the Truth Is So Hard

Naming abuse means we can't un-know it. When they show you who they really are, believe them. Admitting we're not safe means we can't keep playing house. Seeing clearly means we have to act. And action is terrifying—because it means change. It means grief. Loss. Starting over. But ignoring it only means more of the same.

Naming the truth didn't erase the pain, but it gave me something solid to stand on for the first time.

### Self-Check: Are You Facing the Truth or Avoiding it?

Have you noticed that anxiety is avoidance's best friend? They are best buds and hang out together all the time.

- Do you minimize what's happening to avoid making a hard decision?
- Do you justify behavior that leaves you feeling confused or hurt?
- Do you self-impose isolation to avoid social events hoping to avoid stress and anxiety?
- Do you fear telling friends or family what's really going on?
- Do you practice escapism – distracting yourself from your unpleasant reality?
- Do you blame yourself for someone else's mistreatment?
- Do you bury your emotions or maybe you aren't even sure if you have emotions anymore?
- Do you say "it's not that bad" even though it *is*?
- Do you fall into wishful thinking imagining conclusions that are great while ignoring your reality?
- Do you practice the Pollyanna Principle where everything is positive, and you forget all the negative?
- Do you use a substance to numb the pain?

If yes, you're not weak. You're human. And you're waking up. You're asking hard questions now—and that means you're already beginning to heal.

## Ways to Reclaim Yourself

Facing the truth is painful. But it's also freeing. Here's how I started facing mine:

1. I stopped calling it "a rough patch." I called it what it was: emotional abuse.
2. I read books, articles, and stories from survivors—I saw myself in their words.
3. I became part of a support group. It's good to know you're not alone.
4. I kept a journal—not to process him, but to understand *me*.
5. I let myself start to feel emotions again and began to learn how to process them.
6. I started recognizing and understanding the reality of my situation.
7. I stopped hoping for him to change and started hoping *I* would make better decisions.
8. I learned to break the 'big' issues down to more manageable bites so I could find solutions.
9. I spoke the truth out loud, even if just in the mirror: "I am not safe here."
10. I learned to reward myself.
11. I found professional help.
12. I started taking care of myself – eating better, exercising, finding quiet time just for me.

The truth hurts, yes. But so does living a lie. When you're ready to face the truth, you're already halfway free.

## Say It. Write It. Own It.

*You don't have to be ready for everything. Just be ready to tell the truth—to yourself. That's how you begin to reclaim your power.*

## Journal Prompt #1:

*What's a truth you tried to avoid in your relationship? What were you afraid would happen if you faced it head-on?*

## Journal Prompt #2:

*Was there a moment, word, or look that finally broke the illusion? Describe the moment clarity hit—and how your body reacted to it.*

## Exercise: Facing the Truth Without Flinching

### Step 1: Complete the Sentence
Write as many endings as you can to this sentence:
"If I'm being completely honest with myself…"

**Example:**
- "If I'm being completely honest with myself… I never felt safe with him."
- "If I'm being completely honest with myself… I stayed because I was scared, not because I believed in us."
- "If I'm being completely honest with myself… I knew something was deeply wrong long before I admitted it."

Let yourself go deep. Don't judge. Just release.

### Step 2: The Cost of the Lie
- Choose one of the truths you uncovered and write:

    *What has it cost me to keep pretending this wasn't true?*

### Step 3: Let the Truth Lead You
- Now ask:

    *If I accepted this truth completely, what would I stop doing? What would I start doing?*

Even if you don't act on it yet, let the answer breathe. This is the beginning of change.

---

*Clarity is painful—but
it's the first real freedom.
You don't owe anyone an explanation.
You only owe yourself the truth.*

*I am strong.*

## Chapter 13

# The Grief That Doesn't Make Sense

For me, grief started when I began to realize the truth. It came quietly—like the ache you feel when you realize someone isn't coming to find you. I can still see him walking silently walking up the stairs, and something in me finally admitted: he's not going to change. He's not the person I thought he could be. That version of him only existed in the future I kept hoping for. And just like that, the future I'd built in my dreams began to fall apart.

Grief doesn't wait for logic. It shows up for the memories, the maybes, the hope you clung to. Even when you know it wasn't healthy, you still mourn what could've been.

### Why Am I Mourning What Hurt Me?

No one tells you that even in the middle of it—even while you're still there—you can grieve what's being lost. People expect clarity. Strength. Relief. Celebration. And yes, you might feel all of that. But also—you'll feel grief. Big, aching, complicated grief.

Because you're not just mourning a relationship. You're mourning the vision of your life you were fighting for.

You might still be in it, still trying, still hoping. Or maybe you've left. Or maybe you're emotionally gone, even if you haven't physically walked out the door. Wherever you are in your process—grief can still find you.

And while you're grieving, people might expect you to feel empowered. You're surviving—shouldn't you be grateful? Shouldn't you be proud and strong? But instead, you feel cracked open. Alone in your sadness. Like no one sees what you actually lost. That loneliness can make you second-guess what's real. But it is real.

Your grief is not a betrayal of healing. It's part of it.

## You'll Grieve What Was Never Real

You'll grieve the good moments. You'll grieve the person they were *sometimes*—the one who seemed to see you, who held you, who knew exactly what to say.

You'll grieve the future you imagined together. The one you clung to when things got hard. The one you defended when people raised concerns.

You'll grieve the idea that it could've worked.

If you had just tried harder.

If they had just meant it.

If love had been enough.

You'll grieve the fantasy—the version of the relationship you *wished* you were in.

You'll grieve the parts of yourself that only showed up when things felt good. The person who laughed freely. The one who thought they were finally safe. The one who made plans.

And hardest of all, you'll grieve the belief that it was ever real love—because part of you still wishes it was.

But now you know: Love shouldn't require you to disappear. It shouldn't leave you second-guessing your worth. It shouldn't come at the cost of your peace. And even if parts of it felt real, you are allowed to grieve the illusion—without needing to return to it.

## Grief Isn't a Sign You Were Wrong

Grief doesn't mean you made the wrong choice. It means something mattered to you. It means you hoped. It means you loved. It means you lost something—even if that "something" was only ever the *potential* of what could have been.

You can grieve a relationship you knew was hurting you. You can grieve the parts of it that felt good. You can grieve even if you were the one who finally chose distance. And you can grieve *even if you haven't left*—because you've still lost something. Grief is not a verdict. It's not proof that you should've stayed or should've left. It's just proof that your heart was fully in it.

And that matters. Because your capacity to feel pain is also your capacity to feel love. To feel hope. To feel healing.

Let yourself feel it. Not because leaving was wrong. Not because staying is wrong. But because letting go is hard—even when it's right.

## The Hardest Goodbyes Happen Inside You

Most people don't see them. They don't hear the quiet endings you carry. But you do.

You say goodbye to the way they used to laugh with you. To the version of them you kept believing would come back. To the inside jokes. The rituals. The small tenderness's that made you hope just a little longer.

You say goodbye to the dreams you kept alive far too long. The trips you planned. The house you imagined. The life you were so sure could still happen if you just held on.

You say goodbye to the part of yourself who believed it would work. Who thought love could fix it. Who thought you could be enough to make them change.

And maybe the hardest goodbye of all? You say goodbye to the version of yourself who didn't know any of this could happen. The innocent one.

The hopeful one. The unguarded one. But you feel every goodbye in your emotions, body, and spirit. That's real. That's grief.

And that loss? It's real. It's deep. It's painful.

No one sees it, but it breaks something. And eventually—*if you let it*—it makes space for something new to grow.

## You Don't Have to Rush Past This

Grief doesn't have a timeline. It doesn't follow a checklist. And it doesn't care how "strong" people think you are.

You don't have to bounce back. You don't have to be okay yet. You don't have to prove you're better because you left—or because you stayed.

This isn't weakness. This is unwinding. This is the exhale after holding your breath for too long.

You were in survival mode. Now you're feeling what you couldn't feel back then. You're allowed to cry over someone who hurt you. You're allowed to miss them, even after what they did. You're allowed to feel angry one minute and shattered the next. You're allowed to still love the good parts and mourn what will never be.

You're allowed to be confused. To not know what comes next. To still want answers. To feel everything—and nothing—at the same time.

Grief isn't the detour. It's part of the road. And it doesn't need to be rushed to be real.

## And One Day—Grief Becomes Grace

It happens slowly. Quietly. The crying doesn't stop all at once. But it comes less often. And then, one day, it doesn't come at all—and you almost miss it.

The ache softens. The memories lose their grip. You stop looking back for answers. You start creating new ones for yourself. You don't forget what happened. But it stops defining who you are.

Grief gives way to clarity. Clarity gives way to peace. And peace gives way to freedom.

## The Grief That Doesn't Make Sense

One day, you wake up and realize:
You're not waiting for them to change anymore.
You're not rehearsing old conversations.
You're not explaining your pain to anyone.
You're just... living.
That's grace. Not a gift from them—a gift you gave yourself.
Not because you tried harder—but because healing found you, when you made room for it.

---

### Self-Check: Are You Grieving Something That Doesn't Make Sense?

Grief after emotional abuse is complicated. It's not always about losing someone—it's often about losing the dream, the hope, the version of life you thought was possible. Whether you've left, or you're still there, you might be grieving without even realizing it.

- You feel deep sadness, even though you know the relationship is unhealthy.
- You miss them and hate yourself for missing them.
- You cry over memories you're no longer sure were real.
- You feel like no one understands the complexity of what you've lost—because it wasn't all bad.
- You replay what could've been, if only they had changed.
- You feel ashamed for grieving when other people think you should "just be over it."
- You're still in the relationship, but already grieving the version of it you hoped for.

- You find yourself nostalgic for the "good moments" and catch yourself minimizing the harm.
- You mourn the version of you who still believed it could work.
- You feel stuck between heartbreak and relief.
- You wonder if grieving means you made the wrong decision—even though you know it doesn't.

Grief doesn't mean it wasn't abuse. It doesn't mean you're weak. It means you've finally stopped pretending it didn't hurt.

## Ways to Reclaim Yourself

You don't have to justify your grief to anyone—not even yourself. You're allowed to mourn what was, what wasn't, and what will never be. Let this be the part where you stop pushing it away.

- Write down everything you feel like you've "lost," even if it feels irrational: dreams, plans, illusions, hope. Let it all be real.
- Say this to yourself aloud:
  *"Just because it hurt me doesn't mean I don't miss it."*
  *"Just because I stayed doesn't mean I wasn't grieving."*
  *"I don't need to explain my grief to feel it."*
- Create a "grief ritual" for one specific goodbye: Light a candle, write a letter, take a walk, say a prayer, cry it out—whatever feels right. Let it mark an ending.
- If you're still in the relationship, acknowledge what you already know is gone. Grieving while staying is valid, too.
- Grief doesn't mean you failed. It means you were brave enough to care deeply.

- Let yourself feel pride for facing this. Grief is not weakness—it's emotional strength in motion.

You don't grieve because you're broken. You grieve because you dared to love, and you're finally telling the truth.

## Say It. Write It. Own It.

*You don't have to rush your healing or have it all figured out. Just honor what was real, grieve what was missing—and reclaim your power one truth at a time.."*

## Journal Prompt #1:

*What are you grieving that others might not understand? Write it without explaining or defending it. Just name what was lost.*

## Journal Prompt #2:

*What do you still miss—and what do you now know was missing? Let those truths sit side by side without trying to resolve them.*

## Exercise: A Letter to What You Lost

### Step 1: Write to the Loss
Write a letter to the dream, the version of them you believed in, or the version of yourself who tried so hard to make it work.
You can start with:
*"I wanted you to be real. I wanted this to last. But…"*
Let the grief speak without interruption.

### Step 2: Let It End
Choose one way to mark this loss—something personal, symbolic, quiet, or loud. Burn the letter. Tear it up. Plant it. Or simply close your journal and whisper, *"It's okay to let this go."*

### Step 3: Speak This Aloud
*"I can love what was good. I can grieve what was missing. And I can move forward anyway —because I deserve peace."*

*Grief is a sign that your
heart still works.
Let it break open—so
something true can begin.*

*I am building a new vision through my grief.*

## INTERLUDE

## The First Time I Told the Truth

I had replayed the past so many times, trying to figure out if I was overreacting or just too sensitive. But there came a day—ordinary, uneventful—when someone asked me if I was okay, and I couldn't lie. I couldn't explain it all. But I heard myself say it, like a whisper I'd been holding for years: "That wasn't okay."

It wasn't a grand moment. There was no big reveal. No speech. No scene. I didn't stand up on a table. I didn't confront anyone. I didn't even cry.

I just said it. Soft. Simple. Shaky. *"That wasn't okay."* And suddenly —I wasn't holding my breath anymore.

### The First Time I Told the Truth, I Thought I Might Break

I was afraid they wouldn't believe me. Or worse—they would. And everything I'd worked so hard to hide would unravel right there. But the unraveling didn't destroy me. It freed me.

It was after a meeting. I thought I was hiding things really well. One of the women stopped me afterward and asked me how I was doing. I gave the standard answer most survivors give, "I'm fine."

She looked at me and said, "No you aren't. Do you want to talk?"
I did. But I didn't.

For privacy we sat in her car. I made a decision. I trusted her —as much as I could trust anyone at that point.

I started telling her a few things. Matter-of-fact. Simple. Statements of behavior. No emotion. Just the facts.

I had no idea if she would believe me. She went to my church. She knew my husband well. How could she receive this? It was a risk.

But because of her training and her work with at-risk youth, she already knew the signs of abuse.

She'd seen them in me. She'd known for a long time —but waited until I was ready. She became a safe place. Not a dumping ground. A refuge. A witness.

## The First Time I Told the Truth, It Was Mostly for Me

I wasn't trying to burn the past down. I just needed to stop pretending I wasn't in pain. I needed someone to see me—not the polished version, not the survivor, not the "I'm fine."

Just me.
Wounded.
Awake.
Honest.

## The First Time I Told the Truth, It Didn't Fix Everything—But It Changed Me

Not all at once. But a crack opened. And light seeped in. And I realized: I didn't need to carry the silence anymore. And I wasn't alone.

The story didn't need to be perfect. It didn't need to be provable. It just needed to be mine.

## The First Time I Told the Truth

The first time I told the truth, I wasn't brave. I was just tired. And sometimes, that's how healing starts.

Maybe your first truth won't be loud either. Maybe it's just a whisper that says, "This isn't love."

That's more than enough to begin.

*I am finding
freedom
in the truth.*

# PART III

# The Return to Myself

*Sometimes, it starts from the inside—*
*long before anyone sees it, there is a shift —quiet, intentional.*

*You stop pretending it doesn't hurt.*
*You stop twisting yourself into a shape that keeps the peace.*
*You stop trading truth for a temporary sense of acceptance.*

*This is where healing begins—not with dramatic exits,*
*but with honest reckonings.*
*Not the performance of strength, but the practice of truth.*
*You grieve what was never real—the good that wasn't good enough.*
*You begin to feel what you once avoided.*
*You look at the damage—and start choosing differently.*

*Here, healing doesn't look heroic. It looks human.*
*You set boundaries and feel guilty.*
*You rest and feel restless.*
*You say no—and cry in the bathroom.*

I Know Who I Am

*But still, you keep going.*
*Piece by piece, you gather what was lost.*
*You stop proving yourself to people who've already made up their minds.*
*You stop trying to fix others and start tending to yourself.*
*You stop disappearing to make others comfortable.*
*You begin choosing yourself, even when it's hard.*
*You don't always recognize who you are becoming.*
*But something in you is waking up—tired, tender, and unafraid of the dark.*
*You realize you're not broken. You're returning.*
*Not to who you were—but to who you are underneath the mask.*

*This isn't the end of pain.*
*But it's the beginning of self-loyalty.*
*You are not going backwards.*
*You are reclaiming your life.*

# CHAPTER 14

# Speaking the Truth Broke Its Power

I was sitting across from a friend as we both enjoyed some pancakes, trying to explain what I hadn't even admitted to myself.

I didn't tell the whole story—I couldn't. But I said one sentence that had been trapped in my chest for years: "This isn't okay."

You can carry a truth for years without speaking it. Especially when the truth threatens to undo your entire identity or cost you the life you've worked so hard to preserve. But the moment it leaves your mouth, everything shifts. Saying it out loud makes it real—and sometimes, that's when the healing begins.

## Telling the Truth Isn't Always a Relief

Everyone talks about the freedom of telling the truth. And yes—freedom is real. But it's not immediate. Sometimes, the first thing that comes after truth… is loss.

Loss of relationships.

Loss of reputation.

Loss of the illusion that you were "fine."

Sometimes, telling the truth means people look at you differently. Or worse—**they don't look at you at all.**

## Truth Has a Cost—And I Paid It

I thought telling the truth would be the end of the pain. But it wasn't. It was the end of the pretending. And that comes with a cost.

You lose people. Sometimes you lose the very people you thought would protect you—and the ones you protected, by staying silent. I lost people I thought were friends. I lost his family who I had known and loved. I lost some of my family. You lose comfort.

It's easier to stay in the familiar pain than to step into the unknown. Even pain can feel like home when you've lived in it long enough. And truth? It's the doorway out—but walking through it means leaving everything familiar behind.

One family holiday dinner, I slipped into the kitchen, the sound of laughter spilling in from the other room, and it hit me—I didn't belong. I hadn't told them everything—just enough to stop pretending. But even that was enough to make me feel like the problem. No one said it out loud. They were acting fairly normal. But something was off. It felt strained. And it stung more than I expected.

You lose your image. The version of yourself you presented to the world—strong, fine, smiling. The one who didn't need help. The one who could handle it.

Telling the truth tears all that down. And not everyone sticks around for what's underneath.

You lose illusions. The hope that maybe it wasn't that bad. The story that maybe they didn't mean it. The fantasy that maybe it could still work.

You lose your silence. And with it, the fragile peace you held by never naming what hurt you. And sometimes, you lose your place.

In your family.

In your friend group.
In a community that doesn't know how to hold hard truths.

It's not fair. But it's real. Truth costs you comfort. But it returns your clarity. And no matter what it takes away, it always gives you this: yourself.

## You Can Tell the Truth and Still Be Afraid

It's okay to let your voice shake. Feel the nausea rise afterward. Wish you could take the words back. Question yourself: "Was it even that bad?"

That's all part of the process. Truth doesn't always come with applause. Sometimes it's met with silence. But truth doesn't need a standing ovation to matter. It just needs to be spoken—and real.

## And Then Something Shifts

The truth is spoken. Their image is no longer protected. Strength stops being a performance. And yes—it costs something: comfort, connection, control. But slowly, something else begins.

You've stopped curating every detail. Managing the narrative has ended. There is no more hiding.

And that shift? It's the beginning of something new. You don't become someone else. Healing begins to shape you into a wiser, braver version of yourself—woven from who you've always been, the journey you lived through, and blossoming into something greater.

## The Truth May Cost You People—But It Will Return You to Yourself

Some people may leave. Some people may get uncomfortable. Some may never understand. But you will.

And that matters more. Telling the truth won't fix everything. But it will free you from pretending. And sometimes, that's all you need to begin again.

### Self-Check: Are You Still Afraid to Tell the Truth?

Telling the truth—especially about emotional abuse—can feel like setting a fire you can't put out. These signs might mean you're still carrying the weight of unspoken truth.

- You rehearse conversations in your head but can't get the words out in real life.
- You downplay or soften your story, so others aren't uncomfortable.
- You're afraid of how people will respond—disbelief, judgment, silence.
- You feel loyal to someone who hurt you, and speaking the truth feels like betrayal.
- You worry people won't believe you unless you have "proof."
- You minimize your experience with phrases like "it wasn't that bad" or "I don't want to make a big deal out of it."
- You haven't told anyone what really happened—not even yourself.
- You fear people will see you differently—or stop seeing you at all.
- You feel more grief or fear about naming the truth than about living inside it.
- You feel responsible for protecting someone who constantly cast themselves as the victim—even though they were the one hurting you.

You don't owe anyone your pain—but you do owe yourself your truth. Even if it shakes things. Even if it costs you.

## Ways to Reclaim Yourself

Start with what's true for you—not what sounds 'right' to anyone else. Telling the truth isn't about getting the perfect words. It's about no longer protecting a story that's hurting you. Start small. Start real. Start where you are.

- Say it to yourself first. Out loud. Without qualifiers. Without disclaimers.
  *"It was emotional abuse."*
  *"I was not safe."*
  *"That wasn't love."*
- Write down the truths you've been too afraid to say. Keep it private—this is for *you*. Let it be messy, unfinished, shaky.
- Choose someone safe—one person—who can hear your story without judgment. You don't need to tell everything. Just begin.
- Stop filtering your pain for other people's comfort.
- Replace *"It wasn't that bad"* with:
  *"It hurt. And that matters."*
- Let go of needing to be believed to tell the truth. Your truth stands even if others never validate it.
- Say this to yourself when you want to retreat:
  *"I'm not breaking the peace. I'm breaking the silence."*

You don't have to shout it. You don't have to set the record straight for anyone else. You just have to stop hiding it and stop rewriting it for yourself.

Truth is the first step back to yourself.

## Say It. Write It. Own It.

*Telling the truth won't always feel safe or clean or clear—but it will always be a step toward freedom. Start with your voice, your page, your truth.*

## Journal Prompt #1:

*What truths have you been holding inside—not because they're not real, but because you're afraid of what will happen if you say them?*

## Journal Prompt #2:

*What do you wish someone had said to you when you first started realizing what was really happening? What would it feel like to say those words to yourself now?*

## Exercise: Write the Unfiltered Truth

### Step 1: Write the thing you've never said
Start with:
> *"The truth I haven't told is…"*

Write as much or as little as you need. Don't worry about how it sounds. Don't protect anyone. This is for you.

**Step 2: Read it back without editing**
Let the truth land—without shrinking from it.
Let it be as raw, sharp, or quiet as it needs to be.

**Step 3: Choose one sentence from it that feels strongest and say it out loud**
Say it to your reflection. Say it to a page.
Say it just once, like a declaration.
> *"That happened."*
> *"It hurt."*
> *"I didn't deserve it."*
> *"I am not protecting their story anymore."*

Let it ring in your own voice.

*You don't need a permission*
*slip to speak the truth.*
*You only need the courage*
*to stop pretending.*

*I am expressing
my truth
fearlessly.*

## Chapter 15

# Realizing It Wasn't My Fault

I would lay awake at night, replaying arguments I didn't start and reactions I didn't understand—trying to pinpoint the moment I "messed up." I kept asking, "What could I have done differently?" I didn't know then that I was asking the wrong question.

Once I could name it, I could finally ask the next question: *Was it ever really my fault?* And for the first time, the answer came back: *no. It wasn't.*

## The Lie We Absorb

No one says it out loud, but the message is everywhere:
*"You must've done something."*
*"You chose him."*
*"You stayed."*
*"You're not perfect either."*

It's subtle sometimes. Sometimes not. But it lands the same way: you start to wonder if you caused it.

I can't even tell you how many times I accepted the blame in various situations and in the relationship as a whole. There was so much chaos and confusion, I couldn't figure out what was going on, so I just blamed myself. If I couldn't make simple decisions, I was probably the problem, right?

## The Blame Creep

It creeps in slowly, like mold on the walls of your memory.

- *"Maybe I provoked him."*
- *"Maybe if I hadn't raised my voice."*
- *"Maybe I overreacted."*
- *"Maybe I am a burden."*
- *"Maybe I wasn't clear enough."*
- *"Maybe I should've stayed calmer so he didn't escalate."*
- *"Maybe I triggered him without meaning to."*
- *"Maybe I should've just tried harder to understand him."*

But here's the truth—

**Abuse is never your fault.**
**Manipulation is not caused by your kindness.**
**Cruelty is not a reaction to your boundaries.**
**You Didn't Cause Their Behavior**

I found myself apologizing for being late—even though I wasn't late at all. I'd left work on time and gotten home at the usual hour. He was upset because he was hungry and I wasn't there to cook a meal exactly when he wanted it. He wasn't even working at the time. He'd been home all day and could've made something himself. Besides, the refrigerator was full of left-overs. But still, I felt like I had failed. That night, I replayed the whole conversation, trying to figure out how I could've handled it differently so he wouldn't get so upset. I didn't realize it then, but I was blaming myself for his reactions.

You could've been quiet, soft, patient, perfect—and they still would've found a way to control, hurt, or diminish you. Because abuse isn't about you. It's about *them*—their need for power, their wounds, their ego. You didn't make them treat you that way. They chose to.

## Yes, You Stayed—But That Still Doesn't Make It Your Fault

Staying doesn't make you responsible. Trying to fix it doesn't make you complicit. Loving someone who harmed you doesn't make you weak.

You stayed because you were scared. Because you were trauma-bonded. Because you believed in love. Because it was complicated. Because you were surviving. None of that makes it your fault.

## It Wasn't Your Job to Prevent Their Violence

Read that again.
> **It wasn't your job to heal them.**
> **It wasn't your job to keep the peace.**
> **It wasn't your job to absorb the damage.**

It's not on you that they didn't know how to love without control—or that they never took responsibility. Being lied to wasn't your fault.

## It's Not Just About Blame—It's About Ownership

Letting go of blame isn't about erasing the past. It's about **refusing to carry what doesn't belong to you anymore.**

Letting go of blame isn't about pretending it didn't happen. It's not about being the "bigger person." It's not about forgiving and forgetting. It's not even about them. It's about choosing *what you carry forward*. Because blame keeps you stuck in the question: *"Whose fault was it?"* Ownership asks something braver: *"What do I deserve now?"*

Blame keeps you circling the pain. Ownership lets you walk out of it. Blame is heavy, and it's loud. Ownership is quiet—but powerful.

Letting go of blame means letting yourself move. Letting yourself heal. Letting yourself have joy again—without asking permission.

You don't have to carry their guilt to claim your own freedom. You don't have to stay in pain to prove it happened. You can put it down. All of it.

> ### Self-Check: Are You Still Holding the Blame?
>
> You may not say it out loud, but if you're still blaming yourself— even subtly—these thoughts and patterns might sound familiar.
>
> - You replay conversations and wonder what you "should have said."
> - You still believe you could've prevented the abuse if you'd just handled things better.
> - You feel more anger at yourself than at the person who hurt you.
> - You minimize what happened by saying, *"It wasn't that bad."*
> - You explain the abuse by saying, *"We were both toxic."*
> - You avoid telling the full truth to others out of embarrassment or shame.
> - You feel like you owe people an explanation for why you stayed.
> - You believe you're not "allowed" to be angry because you weren't perfect either.
> - You find yourself defending them more than you defend yourself.
>
> Letting go of blame isn't letting them off the hook— it's stepping down from the punishment that was never yours.

## Ways to Reclaim Yourself

You can't rewrite the past—but you can stop letting it define who you are. Letting go of blame isn't weakness. It's clarity. It's freedom. It's yours.

- When the shame spiral starts, pause and say:
  *"What happened to me wasn't my fault. I did what I had to do to survive."*

- Write down every reason you blamed yourself—and then write a compassionate truth next to each one.
  Example:
  *"I should've seen it coming."* → *"It wasn't clear until it was too late—and that's not on me."*
- Practice replacing "I should've known" with "Now I know."
  The first keeps you stuck. The second moves you forward.
- Name what *was* your responsibility—and what wasn't.
  Let that boundary be the beginning of self-protection.
- Say this out loud:
  *"Their choices were never about me. My pain is valid. And I don't have to carry their consequences anymore."*

**You didn't deserve it. You didn't cause it. And you don't have to keep reliving it to prove it was real.**

## Say It. Write It. Own It.

*You don't have to keep proving how hard it was. You just have to stop believing it was your fault.*

I Know Who I Am

## Journal Prompt #1:

*What are some specific things you've blamed yourself for in this relationship? List them without judgment. Then, next to each one, write what you would say if someone you loved told you the same story.*

## Journal Prompt #2:

*What would your life feel like if you no longer had to carry the weight of that blame? Write freely—no guilt, no qualifiers, just possibility.*

## Exercise: Drop the Weight

### Step 1: Write the Blame List
Write a list titled: *"What I Thought Was My Fault."*
Get it all down—every "should," "if only," and "maybe it was me."

### Step 2: Cross It Out
Now, go line by line and cross out what no longer belongs to you.
You can write beside it: *"Not mine."* Or *"I release this."*
Or simply draw a bold line through it like a boundary on paper.

### Step 3: Write This Instead
At the bottom of the page, write:
*"I didn't cause it. I couldn't control it. I don't have to carry it."*
*"It was never my fault."*
Say it aloud. More than once. Let it land.

*Self-blame is heavy.*
*Truth is lighter.*
*Let this be the chapter where*
*you finally put it down.*

*I am
blameless.*

## Chapter 16

# I Didn't Need to Be Perfect to Be Forgiven

I used to think forgiveness meant saying it didn't hurt—or pretending it didn't matter anymore. Forgiveness felt like saying what had happened was okay. But I couldn't keep doing that. I had spent years trying to move on without ever really acknowledging what happened. The turning point wasn't a moment of grace for someone else. It was the first time I looked at myself with tenderness instead of blame.

Forgiveness isn't about excusing what hurt you. It's about meeting the parts of yourself that survived—and choosing to love them anyway.

## The Shame Comes After

No one tells you this: After you begin to heal, after you survive the chaos, after you start to breathe again—the shame shows up. Not their shame. Yours.

You re-play every red flag. Every conversation. Every chance you had to walk away. You might even read old texts or emails that now glare with truth you couldn't see back then. I did.

You whisper to yourself:
*"Why didn't I just leave?"*
*"Why did I ever think this would work?"*
*"Why didn't I just say no?"*

And the voice in your head—sometimes your own, sometimes one you inherited—calls you weak, naïve, stupid. But here's the truth:

You weren't weak. You were surviving.

You weren't blind. You were taught to see love as pain.

You weren't broken. You were exhausted and in need of safety.

You weren't too trusting. You were taught to give people the benefit of the doubt.

You weren't the problem. You were inside one.

## What You Were Up Against

Abuse doesn't usually start with screaming. It often starts with charm—warmth, connection, the illusion of safety. You didn't walk into the fire. The path looked like care and safety. What seemed like love slowly became control. Over time, the volume lowered, the effort increased, and the sense of self quietly slipped away.

He was so personable, with a boisterous, infectious laugh. By the time I realized he only used those traits to reel people in, I was already under his control—drowning my own needs to keep him happy.

That's not failure. That's what happens when someone erodes your trust, your identity, and your sense of what's real.

## Of Course You Stayed

I stayed because I didn't really know any better. I've told you about my authoritarian father. But not about my mother. She had all the signs of a deeply controlling and manipulating person. I didn't see it—*not for most of my life*. Being with someone controlling felt familiar. I didn't like it, but it felt like home.

Until it didn't.
Until I realized:
*That's not how life is supposed to be.*
And there were other reasons, too—maybe some you recognize:

- You believed in them.
- You didn't want to give up on love.
- Your nervous system was hijacked by trauma bonds.
- You thought love meant loyalty.
- No one taught you what abuse without bruises looks like.
- You were still trying to be "good."
- You were human.

Maybe you're still in the process of untangling what's true. What matters is this: you've begun to see clearly. You've started coming back to yourself. And that alone is powerful. That alone is enough. Truth doesn't demand you to leave—it invites you to awaken.

## You Don't Need to Keep Punishing Yourself

You've already lived it. You don't need to keep reliving it. Compassion doesn't have to be earned through constant penance. You can honor yourself for surviving with the tools you had. You can thank yourself for finding a way through. You deserve mercy—not punishment. And perfection was never the requirement, only love.

**Forgiveness isn't about saying it was okay.**
Forgiveness is about choosing not to carry it anymore. You don't have to excuse what they did. You don't have to reconcile. But holding on will keep you stuck, and releasing them through forgiveness is an act of freedom—not for them, but for you. Forgiving doesn't mean forgetting. It means refusing to relive their harm so you can reclaim your peace.

## Forgiveness Isn't Forgetting

Forgiving yourself isn't pretending you weren't hurt. It's honoring that version of you who did what they had to do to get here. It's saying: *"You did the best you could with what you had. I see you now. And I forgive you for not knowing what you couldn't have known."*

> ### Self-Check: Are You Still Carrying the Shame?
>
> Where guilt says *"I **did** something wrong,"* shame says *"I **am** something wrong."* Shame whispers that you should've known better. But what if compassion speaks louder? Let's find out where blame is still living inside you.
>
> - You constantly replay past moments.
> - You talk to yourself in a way you'd never talk to a friend.
> - You feel embarrassed or angry when you think about how long you lived like that.
> - You feel like you have to earn your own forgiveness.
> - You don't share your story fully because you still feel responsible.
> - You assume people will judge you the way you judge yourself.
> - You feel stuck between anger and guilt.
>
> You can't hate yourself into healing. You have to love the person who didn't know better—because they are the one who got you here.

## Ways to Reclaim Yourself

Forgiveness doesn't erase the past—it releases you from punishing yourself for it. Start by showing up for yourself the way you needed someone to back then.

- Write a letter to the version of you who stayed—and only speak to her with love.
- Practice saying, "I didn't know what I know now. That doesn't make me weak—it makes me human."
- Interrupt shame spirals with compassion: "I'm not going there today. I'm healing."
- Share your story with someone safe—and let them hold space without fixing you.
- Speak the words: *"I see you. I forgive you. You did what you had to do."*

You don't need to keep proving you've healed. You just need to stop apologizing for having survived.

## Say It. Write It. Own It.

*Let this be the moment you stop apologizing for how you survived. You've carried the weight long enough—now give yourself a voice.*

## Journal Prompt #1:

*What do you still blame yourself for? Write down the thoughts that loop in your mind—the ones that still carry judgment, guilt, or regret.*

## Journal Prompt #2:

*Imagine someone you love went through exactly what you did. What would you say to help them feel safe, seen, and forgiven? Now offer that same truth to yourself.*

## Exercise: A Letter of Forgiveness

### Step 1: Write to the One Who Endured
Write a letter to the version of you who kept going, who stayed silent when you needed support, who endured what you now see more clearly. Use her name if you want. Be honest. Be kind. Start with:
*"I know why you endured. I see what you were up against..."*
Tell yourself what you couldn't know at the time. Tell yourself what you did right. Tell yourself you're still lovable. That you're not to blame.

### Step 2: Burn the Scorecard
Make a list of the things you think disqualify you from healing, freedom, or love.

# I Didn't Need to Be Perfect to Be Forgiven

Then write next to each one: *"This does not make me unworthy. This makes me human."*

You can tear it up. Burn it. Bury it. Or just close the journal. Let that list go.

**Step 3: Reclaim Your Story**

Complete this sentence 3–5 times:

*"I used to believe I was _____ because I endured. Now I know I was _____."*

Examples:
- "I used to believe I was pathetic because I endured. Now I know I was loyal, scared, and doing my best."
- "I used to believe I was weak. Now I know I was surviving."

*Self-forgiveness isn't earned—it's allowed. You are allowed to stop punishing yourself for how you made it out alive.*

*I am worth forgiving.*

INTERLUDE

# The Masks I Wore

I didn't always know I was hiding. Sometimes I thought I was just surviving. So I smiled. I helped. I held it all together. I was the capable one. The strong one. The one who always bounced back.

No one saw the panic behind my composure.

No one saw the exhaustion in my competence.

No one saw the grief buried under the "I'm fine."

But I wasn't lying—not exactly. I was performing safety. Performing love. Performing okay. Because somewhere along the way, I learned that being too honest—too sad, too angry, too real—was dangerous. That if I showed up as I really was, I might be more than could be accepted. I might be rejected. I might be punished. I might not be loved.

So, I wore the mask.

And at first, it protected me. But eventually, it started to erase me. I forgot what I looked like underneath. I forgot what it felt like to tell the truth before editing it. I forgot how to cry without apologizing for it. I forgot how to be with people without performing strength. I forgot how to be vulnerable without fearing it would cost me acceptance.

It makes me wonder now—

I Know Who I Am

> *What mask did I wear to stay safe?*
> *Who was I trying to be… so that I wouldn't be left?*

And more importantly—

> *What part of me was I hiding?*
> *What part of me still wants to be seen?*

Because underneath the mask, I was still there —still real, still whole, still worthy of being loved for who I actually was. And when I started to peel it back—slowly, bravely—I didn't lose everything.
 I began to find what was real.
 I began to find myself.

*I am more
than any mask
I wore.*

## Chapter 17

# When I Finally Stopped Hiding

I used to hide mirrors. I stopped checking my reflection before work—not because I was in a rush, but because I couldn't bear to see the person looking back at me. The spark was gone. The light in my eyes had dimmed. I didn't feel strong or beautiful or even real. I had become a stranger to myself. I couldn't quite name it yet, but something in me knew: I had disappeared. And slowly, I began to wonder if I could find myself again.

When you stop hiding, you begin to grow into the truest version of yourself—the one that's been waiting beneath the fear. Not the version that performed or pleased, but the one that has always been quietly waiting underneath it all.

## It Doesn't Happen All at Once

You don't suddenly wake up loud and fearless. You don't rip the mask off in one dramatic moment.

It starts with a whisper. A no you don't explain. A truth you don't walk back. A story you tell, not for validation—but for yourself.

And suddenly… you're not hiding anymore.

## You Stop Editing Yourself for Other People's Comfort

You stop rehearsing your words before you speak. You stop swallowing your opinions to keep the peace. You stop pretending you're fine when you're hurting. You stop:

- Laughing at jokes that make you uncomfortable.
- Letting people interrupt you and pretending it's no big deal.
- Agreeing with things just to avoid being "too difficult to be around" or "too sensitive."
- Changing your tone to seem less "emotional."
- Smiling when you want to scream.
- Explaining your boundaries like you're asking for permission.

You stop diluting your truth, so other people don't have to feel awkward about your reality. You stop treating your voice like it's a problem that needs to be softened.

You stop editing yourself into a more digestible version of you. And yes—it's scary. It feels like walking into the world without armor. Because it is.

But it also feels like breathing. Like *finally* being in your own skin. And maybe for the first time, you're not worried about being liked. You're focused on being real.

## Now You're Choosing You

You're not trying to be fearless. You're choosing honesty—even when it's uncomfortable. You're choosing tension over silence. Truth over performance. You're choosing you.

You're choosing:

- **Silence** when it's sacred, not when it's scared.
- **Saying no** without softening it to make it more palatable.

- **Being alone** over being tolerated.
- **Living out loud** over staying invisible.

You're no longer working so hard to be "reasonable," "easygoing," or "low-maintenance." You're no longer negotiating with your own needs in the hope that someone else will finally meet them.

You're choosing you. Fully. Not the filtered version. And it's hard. It costs you people. It costs you peace. It might even cost you your old identity. But now—you'd rather be honest and hurting than perform your life for an audience who never really saw you.

You're not being difficult. You're being true. And that's different. You don't feel powerful. You feel raw. But raw is real. And real is strong.

## You Start Meeting Yourself Again

You start hearing your own voice—unfiltered, unedited, unafraid. You listen to your gut and stop dismissing it as overreacting. You remember what your laughter sounds like when it's not nervous or performative.

You remember what it feels like to be in a room and not shrink. You stop asking for approval before making a choice. You stop seeking permission to be the real you. You stop flinching at your own reflection. You remember:

- What you like to wear when no one's judging.
- What music moves you.
- What foods you crave.
- What lights you up when no one is watching.

You get curious again. You try things you forgot you loved. You let yourself want more—without guilt. You let yourself rest—without shame. And slowly, the self you thought was lost? That person isn't gone. They've just been waiting.

You realize you're not broken—you were just buried. And now, piece by piece, you're digging yourself out. And you start saying, *"This is me."*

## It's Not About Being Loud—It's About Being Whole

This isn't about shouting. It's not about being the boldest or the biggest or the bravest in the room. It's about being honest. Being present. Being fully yourself—even when it's uncomfortable.

You're not here to perform. You're not here to convince. You're here to **exist**—without apology.

You stop choosing visibility as a performance and start choosing authenticity as a return. You stop needing to be liked in every room. You stop shrinking in the name of being "easy to love." You stop waiting for someone to validate who you are.

You become someone who takes up space—not because you demand it, but because you finally know you deserve it.

Because when you lay down the mask, you don't become more visible . You become real. And real is everything. When you live as your true self, you stop waiting for someone else to see you. You finally see yourself. And that's where freedom begins.

---

### Self-Check: Are You Still Hiding Parts of Yourself?

Hiding doesn't always look like silence. Sometimes it looks like editing, softening, smiling, overexplaining, or disappearing in plain sight. These signs may mean you're still playing small to stay safe.

- You ask for advice before trusting your own instinct.
- You wait to see how others react before you speak your truth.
- You say "I don't care" when you do—because you're afraid of being judged for having feelings.

- You water down your opinions, creativity, or joy to make others comfortable.
- You worry people won't like you if you show the full, unfiltered you.
- You hesitate before saying what you really feel—and sometimes change your mind.
- You feel guilt or anxiety when you set a boundary.
- You notice that in some spaces, you're a version of yourself—not the whole.
- You crave being fully seen, but you're also terrified of what people will do with your truth.
- You apologize for things that don't need apologizing.
- You overexplain to avoid being misunderstood.
- You tone down your passion, so you won't be called "intense."

You're not being dramatic. You're protecting yourself. But now—you get to protect your truth, too. And that starts by letting it be seen.

## Ways to Reclaim Yourself

You don't have to show up boldly to be seen—you just have to show up as yourself. Start where you are. Let yourself be visible in small, honest ways.

- Finish this sentence in your journal or aloud:
  *"If I weren't afraid of being judged, I would..."*

- Choose one space this week where you'll stop editing yourself. It could be a text, a conversation, your outfit, or the way you share something creative.
- Practice saying something you believe without cushioning it. No disclaimer. No "just my opinion." Let it land.
- Ask yourself:
  *"Is this choice mine—or is it who I think they want me to be?"*
  Then choose again if you need to.
- Make a "Me List":
  Write down things that feel like the real you—books, colors, ideas, music, foods, memories. Reclaim one today.
- Say this to yourself when you feel the urge to shrink:
  *"I'm not here to be small. I'm here to be whole."*

You don't have to become someone new to be free. You just have to stop hiding who you already are.

## Say It. Write It. Own It.

*No more hiding. No more rehearsing. Just you—and the truth. You're not here to disappear. You're here to exist, fully and unapologetically.*

## Journal Prompt #1:

*What part of yourself have you been hiding, shrinking, or softening to fit in, be loved, or stay safe? What would it feel like to let that part breathe again?*

## Journal Prompt #2:

*What does "being fully yourself" mean to you—without performance, apology, or permission? What would one small act of that look like today?*

## Exercise: Stop Editing, Start Showing Up

### Step 1: Write an "unedited" list of things you love, believe, or want—without worrying how they'll be received.
It might look like:
> "I love being direct."
> "I want deep connection."
> "I don't want to be quiet anymore."
> "I'm tired of being palatable."
> "This is me. I'm not sorry for it."

### Step 2: Pick one thing from your list and express it—today.
Say it, write it, wear it, post it, own it.
Let the world meet one more piece of the real you.

### Step 3: Anchor it in your voice
Speak this to yourself in the mirror or journal it:
*"I'm not hiding anymore—not from them, and not from me."*

I Know Who I Am

*You only owe yourself the freedom to be whole—not a smaller version of you for the world.*

*I am confident.*

## Chapter 18

# Self-Love Felt Too Far – So I Started With Self-Respect

I remember driving to work, trying not to cry—not because of anything dramatic, but because I had finally said, "No."

He was trying to spin another tall tale, weaving a story I knew wasn't true. But that day, I decided I wasn't going to let him twist the truth and make me feel like I was losing my grip on reality. So I challenged it—just a quiet, steady: "No, that isn't what happened." And then I walked away.

My hands trembled. My voice shook. But something inside me stayed firm. I wasn't being mean. I wasn't being selfish. I was being honest—and for the first time, I didn't apologize for it.

Loving myself felt like too much to ask. But respecting myself? That I could reach for—one boundary, one truth, one deep breath at a time.

### Self-Love Felt Too Far—So I Started With Self-Respect

People told me to love myself. As if that were easy. As if that were obvious. As if I hadn't already tried. I wasn't even sure what that even meant. Was I supposed to look in the mirror and say affirmations I didn't believe? I could barely look in a mirror at all. Was I supposed to feel radiant and whole after years of being made to feel the exact opposite? That seemed impossible.

The truth is—I didn't feel lovable. I didn't feel beautiful, strong, or wise. I felt tired. Foggy. Ashamed. I felt like someone who had let herself down. Someone who had been missing too long. Someone who had been broken in ways they couldn't name. And when I heard people say, "Just love yourself," it felt like one more thing I was failing.

So I didn't start with self-love. I started with something smaller. Something quieter. But just as powerful.

Self-respect.

It didn't require me to feel good. It didn't require me to believe I was worthy yet. It just asked me to act like I was. One boundary. One truth. One deep breath at a time.

## **Self-Esteem Is How You Feel About Yourself. Self-Respect Is How You Treat Yourself.**

I still had self-esteem in some areas. I was competent. Intelligent. Capable. People admired me. I knew I was good at what I did. But when it came to how I allowed myself to be treated? That esteem disappeared.

Because self-esteem is conditional. It wavers with mood, performance, and perception. But self-respect? That's a choice.

You don't have to feel confident to set a boundary. You don't have to feel worthy to walk away. You don't have to feel strong to say "no." You just have to act like you matter—even if you're not sure yet.

## Self-Respect Sounds Like This

Self-respect started as a whisper. But slowly, it became a voice I trusted. And it sounded like this:

It sounds like saying, *"That's not okay with me,"* even when your voice shakes, even when you're worried they'll leave, even when you're not used to setting limits.

It sounds like, *"I don't owe you my silence,"* because silence protected them, not you. And you're done disappearing to keep the peace.

It sounds like, *"I deserve to be spoken to with care,"* not because you're flawless, but because you're human. You matter, even when you're messy.

It sounds like, *"I will not argue about my worth,"* because your value isn't up for debate—and love that requires you to prove yourself isn't love.

It sounds like, *"I'm allowed to take up space,"* even if someone else finds it inconvenient. Even if you were trained to shrink.

It sounds like, *"I may not feel strong, but I will not abandon myself again,"* because *staying with yourself* is a radical act of recovery.

Self-respect is quiet. Firm. Steady. It may not be loud—but it's non-negotiable.

## Self-Respect Isn't Always Loud

It doesn't always look like confrontation. Sometimes, it's closing your phone and walking away. Sometimes, it's choosing not to explain your boundaries for the hundredth time.

It's choosing quiet over conflict that won't go anywhere. It's not attending the argument just because you were invited.

It's letting them think you're difficult or cold or selfish—because your peace matters more than their approval. It's knowing you don't need to be understood to be whole.

Self-respect isn't about volume. It's about direction—turning inward and asking, "Does this honor me?" And if the answer is no, letting that be enough.

## Self-Respect Doesn't Wait for Self-Love

People say, *"You have to love yourself first."* But what if you don't yet? What if your self-love is still buried under shame, silence, and history? Then you start with what you can reach: Self-respect.

You don't have to feel radiant or confident. You don't have to feel brave or certain. You just have to make a different choice. A choice to:

- Walk away from the thing that hurts.
- Say no without justifying it.
- Rest instead of proving.
- Tell the truth, even if you tremble.
- Ask for space, not because you're angry—but because you're allowed to have needs.
- Stop chasing people who only love the version of you that stays quiet.
- Stop apologizing for your healing taking time.
- Set a boundary even if your voice shakes.
- Believe yourself—even when no one else does.

You don't have to love yourself to protect yourself. You only need to believe you're no longer willing to betray yourself. And sometimes, that's the door self-love walks through. You don't need to wait until you feel worthy to act like you are. Respect comes first. Love grows from there.

---

### Self-Check: Are You Waiting for Self-Love Before You Act Like You Matter?

You don't have to feel worthy before you start treating yourself like you are. Self-respect doesn't require confidence—it just requires choice.

- You know you deserve better, but you still say yes when you want to say no.
- You keep explaining yourself to people who are committed to misunderstanding you.

## Self-Love Felt Too Far – So I Started With Self-Respect

- You minimize your pain because you're not sure you have a "right" to it.
- You wait until you're certain before setting a boundary—because you don't trust your first instinct.
- You fear that prioritizing yourself will make you selfish, dramatic, or cold.
- You don't call something mistreatment unless it's extreme.
- You withhold care from yourself until you've "earned" it.
- You talk to yourself in a way you'd never speak to someone you love.
- You've been trying to *feel* self-love before *choosing* self-respect.

You don't need to love every part of yourself to stop betraying yourself. You just need to stop participating in your own erasure.

## Ways to Reclaim Yourself

You don't need to wait for full self-love to start making different choices. You only need to stop treating yourself like you don't matter.

- Think of one moment this week when you abandoned yourself—when you said yes to something that drained you, softened the truth to avoid conflict, or stayed quiet when something crossed a line.
  Write it down. No shame—just clarity.
- Finish this sentence:
  *"If I respected myself right now, I would…"*
  Don't overthink it. Let the truth rise.

- Choose one small act of self-respect today.
  It could be saying no. Turning off your phone. Resting without guilt. Walking away without explaining.
  You don't need a grand gesture. You just need a beginning. Let it be real—even if it's small.
- Make a "Not Anymore" list:
  List behaviors, people, or patterns you're no longer willing to participate in—not because you feel powerful, but because you're done betraying yourself.
- Practice this out loud:
  *"I may not love myself yet. But I will not disrespect myself anymore."*
  Respect isn't the finish line. It's the doorway. You don't have to feel ready to walk through it.

## Say It. Write It. Own It.

*You don't have to feel ready—just start choosing differently. Let this be the moment you stop waiting to feel worthy and start treating yourself like you are.*

## Journal Prompt #1:

*Where in your life are you waiting to "feel worthy" before you make a change? What would shift if you chose self-respect first?*

**Journal Prompt #2:**

*What does it look like when you betray yourself in small, quiet ways? What would it look like to stop—just once?*

## Exercise: A Promise to the One Who's Still Learning

**Step 1: Write a letter to the version of you who doesn't feel lovable yet.**
Tell her what you're choosing anyway.
Speak to her with tenderness, not pressure.
Let it start like this:
*"You don't have to love yourself yet. But I'm going to start treating you like someone worth loving."*

**Step 2: Choose one phrase of self-respect to keep with you this week.**
Write it on a card. Say it out loud. Let it settle in your body, mind, and spirit.

**Examples:**
- *"I'm allowed to take up space."*
- *"I won't abandon myself."*
- *"I can act like I matter, even if I don't feel like it yet."*

You don't need to believe the whole sentence yet. You just need to stop arguing with the part of you that wants to be free.

# I Know Who I Am

*Self-love is a journey.*
*Self-respect is a choice.*
*And you're allowed to choose*
*it—right now.*

*I am deserving
of respect
and love.*

## Chapter 19

# Learning to Trust Myself Again

Self-respect opened the door—but learning to trust myself again was the harder part. After all the gaslighting and doubt, listening to my own voice felt risky... and sacred.

I remember once standing in the grocery store, staring at rows of various kinds of meat—completely frozen. Me, not the meat. Not because I didn't know what I wanted, but because I wasn't sure if I was *allowed* to want it. Some fish or chicken would taste so good, but we had to eat beef and pork. What if I went to the trouble of cooking it and he refused to eat it – pushed it aside and went looking for a pork chop.

Every decision, no matter how small, came with second-guessing. What if I was wrong? What if I was overreacting? What if I regretted it?

I had spent so long being made to feel I couldn't be trusted—not with money, not with memories, not even with my own emotions—that I started to believe it. Gaslighting doesn't just make you doubt what happened. It makes you doubt yourself.

But deep down, there was a flicker of something still alive. A whisper that said, *"You know more than you think you do."*

That voice was quiet at first. But it was mine. And learning to trust it again changed everything.

## The Scariest Part Was Me

When I let go of denial and started living in the truth, I expected the grief. I expected the anger. What I didn't expect was to be terrified… of myself. I didn't trust my own judgment anymore. How could I?

I'd ignored the red flags. Rationalized the pain. Stayed missing, even when others tried to bring me back. Tried to turn the lies into love — because believing them felt safer than facing the truth.

So the scariest question wasn't, *"Will someone hurt me again?"* It was, *"What if I let them hurt me again?"*

## When Self-Doubt Becomes Your Default

After abuse, your body becomes alert to danger—but your mind questions everything.

- Am I overreacting?
- What if I'm the problem?
- What if I'm broken and I just don't know how to love right?
- What if I lose people because I finally trust myself?
- *What if I never see the signs in time again?*
- What if peace is real, and I still don't know how to receive it?
- *What if my "gut" is just trauma dressed up as intuition?*
- *What if I can't tell the difference between safe and familiar?*

You question your feelings. Your memory. Your needs. You even question the good things—peace, kindness, stability—because they feel unfamiliar.

That's not weakness. That's a nervous system in recovery.

## Sidebar: Your Body Isn't Betraying You

*Before we talk about rebuilding trust, there's something important you need to hear about your body...*

*If you've ever found yourself overreacting to something small—or underreacting to something dangerous—there's a reason. Emotional abuse doesn't just hurt your feelings. It rewires your nervous system. When you're constantly walking on eggshells, your body adapts. You stay on high alert. You brace for impact. You might have numbed out just to get through.*

*It's not weakness. It's survival.*

*Whether you're still in the relationship or not, your body may keep reacting as if you're still in danger. That doesn't mean you're broken. It means your body needs time—and safety—to learn it can soften again.*

*So if you flinch at kindness, or shut down when you're overwhelmed, or can't explain why you're suddenly anxious... you're not failing. You're healing.*

*Your body is trying to protect you. You don't have to fight it. You can learn to listen to it—and slowly, gently, remind it that you're safe now.*

## Learning to Trust Again Starts With You

No one else can rebuild that trust for you. You have to do it with yourself.
That means learning to:

- Hear your inner voice again.
- Believe your gut.
- Validate your needs without outside approval.
- Make small choices and trust they're enough.
- Stop outsourcing your safety.

## Small Decisions, Big Trust

You don't rebuild trust by making one big, perfect choice. You rebuild it by making dozens of small ones:

- Choosing your own food, not what someone else likes.
- Going to bed when *you* feel tired.
- Saying "no" without apologizing.
- Speaking up—even when your voice shakes.
- Not texting back—and being okay with the silence.

Every time you make even the smallest choice for yourself, you send a message to your mind, body, and spirit:
*I'm safe now. I've got me.*

## You Don't Have to Be 100% Sure to Take the Next Step

You won't feel ready. You won't feel certain. That's okay. You only need to believe this:

*I trust myself enough to try again.*
*And if I get it wrong, I trust myself to recover.*
*I am no longer afraid of me.*

---

### Self-Check: Are You Rebuilding Self-Trust?

Self-trust doesn't arrive all at once—it returns in whispers and small choices. Here's how you might know it's starting to come back.

- You set realistic goals.
- You practice self-care.
- You show yourself kindness.

- You reward yourself.
- You listen to you.
- You hesitate less when making everyday decisions.
- You pause and ask yourself what *you* want—and sometimes you even honor it.
- You feel resistance to people-pleasing—and you're starting to listen to it.
- You no longer need someone else to confirm what your gut already knows.
- You notice discomfort in your body and treat it as information, not drama.
- You give yourself permission to slow down, say no, or walk away.
- You stop second-guessing your version of events just because someone disagrees.
- You've started to believe that the old you wasn't stupid—just hurt.
- You honor and give space to your emotions.
- You learn to forgive yourself.

Rebuilding trust with yourself isn't instant—it's a daily reunion.

## Ways to Reclaim Yourself

You don't have to be perfectly confident to begin trusting yourself—you just need to stop abandoning yourself in the moment.

- Make one decision today without asking for outside validation. Start small.
- Keep a journal of your gut feelings—each time you sense something isn't right or feels off, record it. Over time, you'll see how often your instincts were guiding you.
- Speak aloud one truth you normally suppress. Even if no one's listening.
- Practice self-validation: *"I hear myself. I believe myself. That's enough."*
- Create a short mantra to return to when you feel shaky:
  *"Even if I doubt, I'll still show up."*
  *"My voice matters."*
  *"I don't need certainty to choose myself."*

Self-trust isn't built by getting it all right—it's built by showing up, again and again, for yourself.

## Say It. Write It. Own It.

*You don't have to be certain. You just have to show up for yourself—again and again.*

## Journal Prompt #1:

*What's one moment from your past where you doubted yourself—but later realized you were right all along? What did your gut know? What would it look like to honor that instinct today?*

## Journal Prompt #2:

*What does your inner voice sound like now? What would change if you trusted that voice completely?*

## Exercise: Relearning to Listen

### Step 1: Talk to Your Gut
Write a short note to your intuition. Yes, really. Start with:
*"Hey, I'm sorry I stopped listening. I didn't know how to trust you back then..."*
Tell your gut what you want now. Speak to that inner voice: you're trying again, you matter."

### Step 2: Decision Practice
Write down three decisions—big or small—you've made recently.
Then answer these questions next to each:
- Did I make this choice based on fear or trust?
- Did I check in with myself before deciding?
- How did it feel in my body after I chose?

Now: circle the one that felt the most honest. That's your new evidence.

### Step 3: Choose One Brave Thing
Pick one decision you've been putting off—something your gut knows, but your fear's been debating.
Write it here. Commit to taking *one small step* toward it this week. It doesn't have to be huge. Just real.

*You don't have to be sure—you just have to be loyal to yourself. Trust isn't a feeling. It's a decision. And now it's yours to make.*

*I am learning to trust myself.*

## Chapter 20

# I Was Protecting Myself from Hurt — And From Help

Once I began to trust myself, I realized how much I'd been protecting myself from everyone else. I wasn't just avoiding pain—I was avoiding possibility. Because letting people in meant doing something scarier than I expected: being seen.

I remember being at a friend's 50th birthday party—surrounded by kind people, laughter, music, and joy. They were dancing and connecting. I sat there feeling like I was behind glass—present, but not part of it.

I smiled. I nodded. But my guard never dropped. Even when someone asked how I was doing, I gave a polished answer, not a real one. It wasn't about them. It was about me. I didn't know how to let anyone see past the surface.

Being known felt dangerous. But staying hidden started to feel even worse.

## Letting People in Again

I didn't just lose myself in that relationship—I lost connection. To others. To safety. To being truly seen.

When someone breaks your trust over and over, it doesn't just make you wary of them. It makes you wary of yourself. I stopped letting people all the way in—not because I didn't want relationships, but because I didn't trust my ability to choose safe people anymore.

I questioned my instincts. I second-guessed my openness. I built quiet walls—smiles on the outside, distance on the inside.

And if I'm honest? Some days, I still do. Trusting others means first rebuilding trust in yourself—and that kind of healing takes time.

## Being Alone Felt Safer Than Risking Connection

I told myself I was better off alone. That I didn't need anyone. But the truth is—I didn't really want to be completely alone. I wanted to be **unhurt.** And being alone felt like the only way to guarantee that.

That independence was my superpower now.

And some of that was true. But some of it was armor. Because after being manipulated, dismissed, or betrayed—connection stopped feeling safe. Letting someone in meant giving them access to my softness. And softness had become a liability.

So I shut the doors. I stopped reaching out first. I learned how to carry it all myself—grief, confusion, healing, even joy.

No one could twist my words if I said nothing or abandon me if I didn't get attached. No one could disappoint me if I kept expectations low. I called it independence. Sometimes it was. Mostly, it was protection.

I told myself I liked the quiet. I told myself I was just "more independent now." I told myself I didn't want to burden anyone.

But what I didn't realize was this: **Isolation protected me from harm, but it also protected me from help.**

And healing—real healing—needs both boundaries *and* connection.

## I Got So Good at Being Unreachable, I Forgot How to Let Anyone Close

Even the safe ones. The ones who asked. The ones who stayed. I told them *"I'm fine."* I turned questions into jokes. I kept my feelings folded up in my chest like a secret I wasn't allowed to tell.

Abuse taught me not to need. Healing taught me how to need safely.

## Part of Healing Is Unlearning That

Abuse taught me to make myself smaller, to expect less, to hide the truth, and to silence myself in the name of safety. It taught me that needing people was dangerous. That closeness meant control. That vulnerability was an opening someone would use against me.

And I believed it.

Because at the time? That belief *kept me alive*. But survival isn't the same as wholeness. Healing meant unlearning the rules I had followed to stay safe. Rules like:

- Don't need too much.
- Don't talk about it.
- Don't expect to be held.
- Don't let them see you cry.
- Don't tell the whole story.
- Don't be the one who cares more.
- Don't ask for what you really need.
- Don't trust the good parts—they're just the setup.
- Don't show your joy—it makes you vulnerable.
- Don't open up. Don't get used to it. Don't get comfortable.

Healing meant rewriting the story: that I could be open *and* protected. Connected *and* powerful. Honest *and* still loved.

Unlearning doesn't happen all at once. But each time I let someone in without shrinking or apologizing, I remind my nervous system: *"This is allowed now. This is safe now. This is different."*

## The First Time I Let Someone In Again, I Felt Exposed

It wasn't some big confession. It was a text I didn't rewrite ten times. A story I told without making myself the villain. A moment when I let the silence stay open—without filling it with false comfort. And it scared me. But it didn't destroy me.

Because I didn't know how they'd respond. And part of me was sure they'd pull away. Or judge me. Or worse—*pretend to understand and secretly not*. But vulnerability isn't weakness—it's choosing connection anyway. Even when fear says shut it down. So, I chose. Guess what?

They didn't do any of those things. They stayed. They nodded. They said, *"That makes sense."*

And I exhaled in a way I didn't know I'd been holding my breath. I expected to feel weak. But I felt real. And real felt stronger than any armor I'd ever worn.

## I Still Don't Trust Easily—But I Trust Myself to Walk Away If I Need To

That's the difference now. I don't need people to be perfect. I need them to be safe. And I need to be safe with myself first. If I get hurt, I'll know what to do. If someone crosses a line, I'll know how to respond. If I feel myself shrinking, I'll choose myself again.

Letting people in isn't about going back to how I used to be. It's about moving forward as someone who knows how to belong to themself—even in a room full of others.

Letting people in again isn't easy. But hiding has never been healing. And this time, I'm choosing connection without self-erasure.

## I Was Protecting Myself from Hurt — And From Help

### Self-Check: Are You Still Keeping People Out?

Sometimes the deepest loneliness doesn't come from being alone—it comes from being surrounded by people who don't really see you. Or from never letting the ones who could, get close enough.

- You say *"I'm fine"* before anyone even finishes asking.
- You only share your truth after you've made it sound manageable.
- You feel safest when you're emotionally self-contained.
- You've told yourself not to need anything from anyone.
- You're the strong one, the listener, the helper—but you rarely let others do that for you.
- You replay interactions where you *almost* opened up and then backed out.
- You avoid vulnerability by being funny, distracted, or busy.
- You've convinced yourself that no one really wants to hold your truth—so you hold it all alone.
- You love deeply but often feel un-held, unseen, or unreceived.
- You crave connection but keep proving to yourself that you don't need it.

You don't have to trade self-protection for self-betrayal. You get to choose connection *and* safety. And you don't have to do it all at once.

## Ways to Reclaim Yourself

Letting people in again doesn't mean spilling everything. It means letting yourself be seen—one truth, one choice, one safe moment at a time.

- Think of someone in your life who feels *safe-ish*. Not perfect. Not pressure-filled. Just… safe enough.
  What would it feel like to share a little more with them than you usually do?
- Finish this sentence:
  *"The thing I never say out loud but wish someone knew is…"*
- Let someone support you in a small way.
  Accept help with a task. Let them pay. Ask for something simple and specific.
- Pause before saying *"I'm fine."* Ask yourself: *"What would happen if I told the truth?"*
  You don't have to say everything. Just don't disappear.
- Write down what connection used to mean to you—and what you want it to mean now.
  This is your new definition. Not theirs.
- When fear says "Don't let them in," respond with:
  *"I get to choose who sees me now. And I choose people who know how to hold me."*

Letting people in isn't about being soft. It's about being seen—and not shrinking.

## Say It. Write It. Own It.

*You're not here to stay hidden. You're here to be known—gently, bravely, one truth at a time.*

## Journal Prompt #1:

*What are you afraid might happen if someone really saw you? What would it feel like if they didn't run?*

## Journal Prompt #2:

*What do you miss about feeling connected—to people, to belonging, to being known? What do you need more of?*

## Exercise: Name Your Safe People

### Step 1: Make a "Safe-ish" list
List the names of people who have shown up for you with gentleness, patience, or consistency—even in small ways.
This isn't a forever list. It's a starting point.

### Step 2: Circle one name
Now write one sentence you could tell them that feels a little closer to the real you.
Something like:
>  *"I've been holding a lot lately."*
>  *"I'm trying to trust myself more these days."*
>  *"I don't talk about it much, but that really hurt."*

I Know Who I Am

**Step 3: Decide what you'll do with that sentence**
Say it. Text it. Journal it.
Let it live somewhere outside your silence.

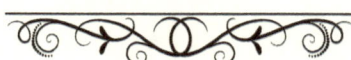

*You don't have to tell everything.*
*You just have to stop disappearing.*
*Let someone meet you*
*where you really are.*

*I am no longer
invisible,
I am becoming
invincible.*

## Chapter 21

# When Being Needed Became My Identity

For years, I thought being needed was the same as being loved. But being the strong one—the reliable one—became a role I didn't know how to stop playing.

I remember once coming home from work late, exhausted after a difficult day. But instead of resting, I cleaned the house, made dinner, and checked to see what he needed. No one asked me to. But no one stopped me either. He used to ask why I never sat down to rest—but if I did, he'd always want something more, so I had to get up anyway. Somewhere along the way, I started believing my worth depended on being the strong one—even when I was falling apart.

## When Caretaking Becomes Your Identity

I was always the one who held it all together. The helper. The responsible one. The one who showed up. The calm in the chaos.

People trusted me. Depended on me. Leaned on me. And I let them. Because it felt like love. It felt like value. It felt like purpose.

But over time, it stopped feeling like connection and started feeling like obligation. Like a performance I couldn't step out of. I didn't know how to ask for help. I wasn't even sure I was allowed to. Somewhere along the way, I forgot that I had needs too—and even if I had remembered, I wouldn't have known how to speak them.

But it wasn't sustainable. And it wasn't safe. Because somewhere along the way, I forgot that I had needs too.

## Caregiving Was My Disguise

I looked selfless. I looked generous. I looked grounded. I looked like I had it all together. But really, I was disappearing. I wasn't helping. I was hiding.

I poured into everyone else to avoid the emptiness inside. I stayed busy to outrun the loneliness I didn't want to name. I took care of people who hurt me—because it was easier than asking why I kept letting them.

Behind every offer to help was the fear of being rejected. Behind every "I've got it" was the belief that *no one would choose me if I stopped performing.* Behind every sacrifice was a part of me that didn't believe I deserved to rest.

I said yes because I didn't know I was allowed to say no. I stayed strong because I didn't believe I was allowed to fall apart. I made myself indispensable because I didn't believe I was lovable without being useful. And it worked—for a while.

People praised me for being the rock. For being so giving. For being so good. But it was goodness at the expense of wholeness. Because while I was showing up for everyone else, I was ghosting myself.

Caregiving gave me a role. But it cost me myself. I made myself small enough to fit inside their needs. And in doing so, I went missing from my own life.

## What I Called Love Was Often Control

If I could meet everyone's needs, I thought I'd be safe. If I just held everything together, maybe I could prevent the next explosion. If I stayed indispensable, I wouldn't be rejected. So, I over functioned. I smoothed things over. I carried the emotional labor of entire relationships. I thought love meant being useful. But it was a role—not a relationship. A performance I perfected out of fear.

And when I finally broke down, people were confused—because I never let them see me struggle. I made myself essential. But I never let myself be seen.

## The Care Came from a Real Place—But the Cost Was Too High

I cared deeply. I still do. But somewhere along the way, caring became a compulsion. A reflex. A mask. It became a way to avoid my pain—a way to earn belonging, to prove I was worth keeping.

But that's not love. That's survival.

And the more I gave, the more invisible I became.

## I'm Still Learning the Difference Between Compassion and Compulsion

Now I ask myself:

- Am I helping because I want to? Or because I'm afraid not to?
- Is this generosity—or is it self-erasure?
- Am I being kind? Or am I managing someone's emotions to avoid fallout?
- Do I feel free to say no—or do I feel obligated?
- Would I still do this if I believed I didn't have to earn love?

- Am I listening to someone—or trying to fix them so I feel worthy?
- Do I feel resentful after giving—or do I feel nourished?
- Am I offering care—or overextending to avoid feeling powerless?
- Do I know what I need right now—or have I only been focused on their needs?

**Compassion is rooted in presence. Compulsion is rooted in fear.**

Love doesn't require you to lose yourself. And care shouldn't cost you your peace.

## I Can Still Care—But I'm Allowed to Come First Now

I'm learning to say no. To rest. To not explain. To let people sit in their own discomfort, instead of rushing in to rescue them.

I'm learning to meet my own needs before I pour into anyone else. And I'm learning that being loved doesn't mean being used.

You are not just a caregiver. You are a person. And you matter—even when no one needs you.

---

### Self-Check: Is Caregiving Costing You Yourself?

Being helpful doesn't make you whole. Being needed isn't the same as being loved. Care becomes harmful when it replaces your identity. If caregiving has become your identity, you may notice yourself doing things like this:

- You say yes even when you're running on empty.
- You feel guilty resting when others still need something.
- You believe your value comes from what you *do*, not who you *are*.

# When Being Needed Became My Identity

- You feel anxious when you're not fixing something for someone else.
- You've made yourself essential in everyone's life—except your own.
- You don't know how to receive the same support you give.
- You feel resentful, but then immediately shame yourself for it.
- You're praised for being strong but secretly wish someone would just care for *you*.
- You feel invisible when you're not in a caretaking role.
- You don't know who you are outside of being useful.

You can still care deeply—without abandoning yourself in the process. You're allowed to come first sometimes. You're allowed to just be.

## Ways to Reclaim Yourself

You can still be kind. You can still show up. You can still care. But you don't have to disappear to do it.

- Think of one recent moment where you overextended yourself.
  Ask: *Was I trying to help—or trying to stay safe, loved, needed, or in control?*
- Finish this sentence:
  *"If I believed I didn't have to earn love, I would…"*
- Choose one situation where you usually step in—and practice stepping back.
  Let them be uncomfortable. Let them figure it out. Let yourself rest.

- Create a "Care for Me" plan.
  What does support look like when it's directed at *you*?
  Where can you ask for help, or give yourself what you so often give to others?
- Start saying this (even just in your head):
  *"I am still good, even when I'm not giving."*
  *"I am still worthy, even when I'm not needed."*
  *"My presence is enough. I don't have to perform."*

You're allowed to lay down what you've been carrying. And the people who love you won't stop loving you when you do.

## Say It. Write It. Own It.

*Your worth was never in how much you gave. It's in who you are—rest, stillness, and all.*

## Journal Prompt #1:

*When did being helpful become part of your identity? What did it protect you from? What did it cost you?*

## Journal Prompt #2:

*What do you believe would happen if you stopped over-giving or over-functioning? What part of that belief is true? What part is fear?*

## Exercise: Write to the One Who Always Gave

**Step 1:** Write a letter to the version of you who gave and gave and gave—until there was nothing left.
Tell them what you see now.
Tell them you understand.
Tell them they deserve rest and care, too.
> Begin with:
> *"You thought being needed would keep you safe. Here's what it really did…"*

**Step 2:** Choose one affirmation to say when you feel the pull to disappear into someone else's needs.

**Examples:**
- *"I can care without sacrificing myself."*
- *"My value isn't measured by how much I give."*
- *"I'm allowed to receive."*

*You're not bad for helping.*
*You're just done being erased by it.*
*And that matters, too.*

*I am worth choosing.
Today I choose me.*

# Chapter 22

# Reclaiming My Power

I remember the first time I chose something just for me —and didn't explain it. He had set up a lunch with someone he called a friend—but he didn't have friends, not really. He had people he used until they were used up. People who thought they were building something mutual, when really, they were being managed and manipulated. I had played along before—showed up, smiled, made conversation like a well-trained prop. But something in me had shifted.

I didn't want to support that kind of behavior anymore. I didn't want to be a dog on a leash, paraded around to keep up appearances. So, I said no. And I didn't go.

No apology. No explanation. Just… no.

And for the first time, that no felt like a yes—to myself.

Power isn't about control. It's about choice. And the moment I stopped letting guilt run my life, I started reclaiming the power I never realized I had.

## I Forgot I Had It

There was a time I couldn't make a simple decision without wondering how he'd react. I apologized for things I didn't do. I kept quiet to avoid setting him off. I shrank myself into someone I didn't recognize—because it felt safer that way.

I thought I had no power. But the truth is:

**I didn't lose it. I gave it away.**

And now, I'm taking it back.

## What Personal Power Really Means

It's not about control. It's not about rage. It's not about becoming hard, unshakable, or untouchable. It's about choice. Ownership. Voice. Boundaries.

It's about knowing: "I get to decide who I am—and what I allow." You don't have to yell to be powerful. You don't have to be fearless to be free. Sometimes, power looks like:

- Saying "no" without overexplaining.
- Leaving the room when you're disrespected.
- Asking for what you need and expecting it to be honored.
- Wearing what makes you feel good.
- Walking down the street like you belong there (because you do).

## What Took Your Power

It wasn't just the abuse that took your power. It was everything that came before it—the quiet conditioning that taught you your power was dangerous.

Messages like:

- Be quiet.
- Be agreeable.
- Don't rock the boat.
- Don't make a scene.
- Make everyone comfortable—even if you're dying inside.

These weren't just rules. They were survival scripts.
But not anymore.

## Taking It Back, Bit by Bit

Reclaiming power doesn't happen in one speech or one moment. It happens in layers.

- When you speak the truth—even when your voice shakes.
- When you stop apologizing for your joy.
- When you leave situations that no longer serve you.
- When you listen to your own yes—and your own no.

## Your Power Isn't Loud. It's Rooted.

It doesn't demand. It doesn't beg. It *knows.*

You don't have to prove anything. You don't have to argue. You just have to own your voice, your time, your space, your story. Because power isn't about being in charge of others. It's about finally being in charge of *yourself.*

---

### Self-Check: Are You Reclaiming Your Power?

You might not feel powerful yet—but these shifts mean you're starting to step back into your own authority.

- You stop asking for permission to take care of yourself.
- You say *"I don't like that"* or *"That's not okay with me"*—and mean it.
- You no longer shrink when someone disapproves of your truth.

> - You choose rest without guilt.
> - You make decisions based on *your* values, not someone else's expectations.
> - You feel your anger—and listen to what it's trying to tell you.
> - You realize silence doesn't mean peace.
> - You stop overexplaining to be "understood" and start protecting your energy.
> - You remember that the old you didn't disappear—that part of you has just been waiting.
>
> You don't have to be loud to be powerful—you just have to stop disappearing.

## Ways to Reclaim Yourself

Reclaiming your power starts with remembering you have a choice—every single day. Even in the small things. Especially in the small things.

- Make a "power list": Write a list of truths that remind you who you are, what you've survived, and what you're capable of. These don't have to be big or dramatic. This is your evidence: you're not powerless. You're powerful—and it's time to own that. They can be simple, powerful reminders like:
    - I got through things I thought would break me.
    - I have a good heart.
    - I keep showing up for myself, even when it's hard.
    - I am learning to say no.
    - I deserve peace.

- These don't have to be big or dramatic. They can be simple, powerful reminders like:
  - Practice saying "No, thank you" boldly, with your whole self behind it—no apology, no explanation.
  - Identify one area where you've felt disempowered—and set a boundary, however small.
  - Start choosing your own preferences again: music, meals, clothes, books, friends.
  - Stand or walk with intention—head up, shoulders back, breath full. Let your body practice being powerful.
- Say to yourself daily:
  *"I am not a burden. I am not a problem. I am a force."*
  You don't have to wait for permission to live as your true self in freedom.

## Say It. Write It. Own It.

*You don't have to feel powerful to be powerful. You just have to start choosing like you matter.*

## Journal Prompt #1:

*Where in your life have you felt the most powerless? What was taken, silenced, or diminished? Name it with honesty—not to stay in the pain, but to reclaim your truth.*

## Journal Prompt #2:

*What would reclaiming your power look like today—not in some ideal future, but right now? What does it feel like in your body when you imagine standing in that power?*

## Exercise: Rewrite the Narrative

### Step 1: "They Told Me / I Was Told…"
Write a list of messages you received—directly or indirectly—that made you believe your power was wrong, unsafe, or unacceptable.

**Examples:**
- *"They told me I was too dramatic."*
- *"I was told not to make a scene."*
- *"They told me anger made me unlovable."*

### Step 2: Now You Speak
After each message, respond with what your truth is *now*.

**Examples:**
- *"My feelings are valid. My voice matters—even if it's loud."*
- *"I am not here to make others comfortable. I'm here to be whole."*

### Step 3: Anchor It in Your Body
Write a short power statement to yourself. One line. Repeat it to yourself every morning this week.

**Examples:**
"I'm not small anymore."
"I don't shrink to be safe."
"I am allowed to take up space—and I do."

*Your power was never lost.*
*It was waiting for you*
*to come back to it.*
*Welcome home.*

*I am powerful.*

INTERLUDE

# The First Time I Felt Free

I didn't know freedom would feel so quiet. No fireworks. No fanfare. Just the soft realization: I don't owe anyone an explanation anymore.

It wasn't dramatic. No big moment. No camera-ready revelation.

It was small. So small I almost missed it.

I was alone—but not lonely.

I was quiet—but not afraid.

I was still—but not stuck.

No one needed anything from me. And for once, I didn't feel guilty for having nothing to give.

My husband was having a sexting affair. I saw the texts come through. Read them. Shouldn't have —but I did. And then I confronted him. You heard me. *I confronted him*. Peaceful. Quiet. Bold. Strong. Shaking so badly inside I could hear my ribs clacking.

He had a ton of excuses. I had more than enough. Nothing changed. He maintained the relationship even though he said he didn't. He sent her gifts and lied about it.

But I felt empowered. I kept my peace. I faced fear. I didn't collapse—I stood strong. Something inside me changed in that moment.

## I Know Who I Am

I think it was freedom. Not the kind that roars. Not the kind you post about. Not the kind that looks impressive from the outside. But the kind that feels like this:

- I didn't brace for backlash after speaking up.
- I didn't explain my "no."
- I wore something I liked and didn't ask myself if it was "acceptable."
- I made a decision without crowd-sourcing it first.
- I laughed—and didn't scan the room to see who was watching.
- I stopped trying to fix what wasn't mine to fix —and gave myself permission to move forward.

Freedom didn't come all at once. It arrived in moments. Tiny cracks in the pattern. Small refusals. Brief silences where I didn't rush to fill the gap. It didn't look like confidence. It looked like choice. It looked like me, choosing not to abandon who I was anymore.

And in those moments, I realized: *This is what it means to belong to yourself again.*

*The first time I felt free,*
*I didn't trust it.*
*But I kept walking.*
*And now, the ground is mine.*

*I am courageous enough to be me.*

## Chapter 23

# Messy, Beautiful, Mine: What Healing Looked Like

Healing isn't a straight line. It's a series of messy, sacred moments—some painful, some powerful—where you stop performing and start choosing yourself, again and again.

I remember the day I got a puppy. He had fought me for years on having a dog, but somehow after fifteen years I got past that one. I was playing with her on the floor, watching her tumble and pounce, and suddenly—I laughed. Out loud. And it startled me. The sound felt foreign. Alien. Amazing. I had no idea how long it had been since I'd laughed a real, full laugh.

For the first time in years, I was finally allowing myself to feel. It wasn't graceful or triumphant. It was raw, real, and mine.

That's what healing looked like that day.

### Spoiler: It's Not Pretty, Linear, or Instagram-Worthy

When people think of healing, they picture sunlight and peace and finally feeling whole. But what does it actually look like?

Here's what it really looks like, behind the filters.

- Crying on your kitchen floor at 2 a.m.
- Flinching at kindness because it feels unfamiliar.
- Re-reading old texts and wondering how you missed the signs.
- Unfollowing people who trigger you—even if they mean well.
- Sleeping twelve hours one night and none the next.
- Feeling powerful one day and shattered the next.
- Saying "no" and then crying in the bathroom because it felt selfish.
- Grocery shopping and realizing you have no idea what you like to eat.
- Throwing out clothes that were never really your style.
- Laughing at something dumb—and then suddenly crying because it felt like freedom.

And if that doesn't look like healing to you—it's because no one told you the truth: healing isn't always graceful, but every messy, quiet, chaotic moment is part of coming back to life.

## What No One Tells You About Healing

Healing isn't always beautiful. Sometimes, it's brutal. It's not a straight line—it's a spiral. And it often feels like you're going in circles... until suddenly, you're not.

## What Healing Actually Looks Like

You don't always recognize it at first. You might wilt before you bloom. You might miss them and still know the dynamic isn't healthy. You might feel raw, untethered, or more emotional than ever—but that's what blossoming sometimes feels like.

Healing can feel like chaos. Like grief. Like a breakdown. But all of that is part of coming back to life.

## What Came Back to Life

Healing didn't come all at once—it returned in flickers. Tiny resurrections. Sacred surprises. I started laughing again, not politely but freely—out loud, from the belly. I danced in the kitchen. I sang with the windows down. I noticed beauty. I cooked meals I actually wanted to eat. I lit candles for no reason at all.

Color came back. Music. Curiosity. The ability to rest without apologizing for it. I rearranged the furniture. I wore things that felt like *me*. I reclaimed silence—not as punishment, but as peace.

These were signs I hadn't just survived. I was living.

## I Did It All

I did all of the above and more. It felt messy and sometimes I questioned myself. Some days were really hard because the more ground I took back the more agitated and desperate his actions became. There would be the love bombing. I used to fall for it but now it just felt empty. There was the gaslighting we talked about making me wonder what reality was.

There was projection where he tried to throw his negative feelings and bad behaviors on me as if I were the one doing them. He would play the poor me victim looking for sympathy right after doing something harmful or vengeful to me. Then he might move to guilt tripping where he would try to get me to do something by trying to make me feel bad for him.

## More Manipulations

There were so many tactics. The more I understood them, the easier they became to spot—and resist. Sometimes, all it took was walking out of the room. Here's what I experienced:

- **Hoovering**: After conflict or distance, he'd try to "win" me back with affection, charm, or promises—just long enough to pull me back in.

- **Breadcrumbing**: He'd offer small crumbs of attention or affection to keep me emotionally invested—then disappear for days, often locking himself in the bedroom and only emerging when I wasn't home or when I couldn't see him.
- **Silent Treatment**: He mastered emotional punishment through long stretches of intentional silence, leaving me unsure of what I'd done wrong.
- **Gaslighting**: He twisted reality, making me question my memory, instincts, and sanity until I wasn't sure what was true anymore.
- **Projection**: He accused me of the very things he was doing—throwing his guilt and bad behavior at me as if I were the one responsible.
- **Victim-Playing**: Right after doing something harmful, he'd turn himself into the victim—looking for sympathy, not accountability.
- **Guilt-Tripping**: He used guilt to manipulate me into doing what he wanted—especially when I started pulling away.
- **Smear Campaigns**: He spread exaggerations or lies about me to justify his behavior and gain allies, while painting me as the unstable one.

The more I named these behaviors, the less they worked. Recognition became my boundary. Naming them helped me trust myself again—and reminded me I wasn't the one twisting the truth. I was being manipulated.

## You Know You're Healing When...

You might not feel "healed," but healing always leaves clues.

- You stop explaining your no.
- You cry and *don't* apologize for it.
- You say what you need—even if your voice shakes.
- You don't respond to the message meant to bait you.

- You stop fantasizing about "the good times" and start remembering what really happened.
- You feel sadness, but it doesn't drown you.
- You feel joy, and you let yourself have it.
- You make decisions without asking for permission.
- You start feeling like someone you actually like again.

At first, naming these tactics made me feel ashamed—how could I have missed it all? But eventually, naming them became power. The more clearly I saw the patterns, the less I blamed myself. This wasn't love. It was control dressed up as closeness. And I wasn't weak—I was surviving the only way I knew how.

Each time I recognized a tactic and chose not to play along, I was reclaiming something—my voice, my clarity, myself. But I was no longer reacting on autopilot. I was starting to choose differently. I was starting to see clearly.

And that's when I realized something had shifted. I was healing—even if I didn't call it that yet.

## You'll Think You're Backsliding—You're Not

There will be days you miss him. There will be days when you doubt yourself. There will be days you feel broken all over again. That doesn't mean you're failing. It means you're healing.

Healing means feeling. And when you've been numb for so long, that can feel unbearable. But the feelings are temporary. Your freedom is not.

## Grief Is Part of the Process

No one warns you how much you'll grieve. Even if it was toxic. Even if you were desperate to escape. Even if everyone tells you "you should be happy now."

You'll grieve the hope or vision you fought for. You'll grieve the time you lost. And you'll grieve the relationship—yes, even if it was abusive. You'll grieve things that don't make sense on paper:

- The hope you held onto for so long.
- The fantasy version of who you thought they were.
- The version of yourself who believed the love was real.
- The years, energy, and self-worth you invested.
- The dream of who you could have been together.
- The comfort of familiarity—even when it was harmful.

## The Grief Doesn't End All at Once

You might even grieve the "highs"—the laughter, the connection, the passion. Because even abusive relationships have moments of light. That's what makes it so confusing. And perhaps hardest of all: You'll grieve the version of you who stayed. The one who tried. The one who bent, broke, and vanished just to survive. But that grief is sacred. It means you're awake now. It means you're feeling again. It means you're honoring what you lost—so you can reclaim what's left.

All of that is okay. It costs something to be whole again. Grief doesn't mean you made the wrong choice. It means you finally made the right one—and you're honoring the loss.

## Self-Compassion Is the New Power Move

For years, I beat myself up for how long I stayed blind. Now, I hold that version of me with tenderness. She wasn't weak—she was surviving. She wasn't blind—she was scared. Healing means replacing blame with compassion for the version of you who did what they had to do to survive.

## What No One Tells You

No one tells you that healing isn't all light and relief—it's confusing, disorienting, and sometimes lonely. It sounds like this:

- You might laugh again—and then feel guilty for it.
- You might finally rest—and wonder if you're being lazy.
- You might feel peace for the first time—and mistake it for emptiness.
- You'll miss the chaos—not because it was good, but because it was familiar.
- You'll miss the person who hurt you—and hate yourself for missing them.
- You'll try to explain your pain—and some people won't get it. Some won't even try.
- You'll outgrow people you once thought you'd never live without.
- Healing may ask you to let go more than once—of hope, of illusions, of what was never yours to hold.
- You'll mourn the version of yourself who didn't make it out sooner.
- You'll still hear their voice in your head—until one day, it's quieter.
- You'll feel completely alone—then realize solitude can be sacred.
- You'll do something brave—and immediately question if you deserve the credit.
- You'll start trusting yourself—and it'll feel like breaking the rules.
- You might want love again—and that might terrify you.
- And eventually—
- You'll laugh without checking who's watching.
- You'll speak without bracing for backlash.
- You'll walk into a room without shrinking.
- You'll stop needing someone to save you—because you already did.

It's a lot to carry—but if any of this sounds familiar, it means you're not just surviving anymore. You're healing in real, powerful, life-changing ways.

You're not behind—you're blossoming. Into someone you've never been allowed to be. And every time you choose truth over silence, you're stepping into the life you deserve. This is how it begins—not with certainty, but with courage.

## Healing Isn't a Finish Line

Healing isn't an arrival—it's a slow blossoming into truth, boundaries, and self-trust. You get rooted. You soften without crumbling. You love without losing yourself. You blossom into someone you trust.

> **Self-Check: Are You Healing, Even If It Doesn't Feel Like It?**
>
> During the healing process it's common to question if you are making any progress or if you are really healing. Remember that it can be a messy time. You may not feel "healed," but healing often looks like ordinary moments filled with quiet strength. The clues are subtle—but they're there. Here are some self-check points:
>
> - You cry for no reason—and realize it's not "no reason."
> - You feel everything more intensely, even joy.
> - You stop romanticizing the past.
> - You changed your vision of the future.
> - You notice when something feels unsafe—immediately.
> - You don't explain your 'no' anymore.
> - You have better emotional clarity.
> - You have times when you bravely leave your comfort zone.

# Messy, Beautiful, Mine: What Healing Looked Like

- You don't need chaos to feel alive.
- Your self-esteem is growing.
- You miss them... but you don't want them back.
- You respond instead of reacting.
- You feel lost sometimes—but not stuck.
- You caught yourself smiling.
- You have days that feel ordinary—and that feels like a miracle.
- If you developed an addiction, you find you no longer need that to numb your trauma.
- You can picture a future without pain in it.

You're not behind—you're blossoming into someone you've never been allowed to become.

## Ways to Reclaim Yourself

You don't have to fix your whole life to be healing. You just have to choose yourself—one honest moment at a time.

- Celebrate the quiet wins—resting, laughing, saying no.
- Keep a "healing journal" of signs that you're growing—even tiny ones.
- Create a list of "things I once thought I'd never do again"—then try one.
- Write yourself permission slips: "I'm allowed to rest." "I'm allowed to not know yet."
- Let go of the idea that healing should look like strength. Let it look like truth.

Healing isn't a return to who you were. It's a homecoming to who you really are —and a step toward the life waiting for you.

## Say It. Write It. Own It.

*You're allowed to bloom in your own time, in your own way.*

## Journal Prompt #1:

*What does your healing look like right now? Be honest. Is it messy, quiet, emotional, confusing, hopeful—or all of the above?*

## Journal Prompt #2:

*What are some things you've grieved that others might not understand? What did those losses mean to you? Why were they significant, even if no one else gets it?*

## Exercise: Track the Clues of Your Healing

### Step 1: Identify the Signs
Make a list of *at least five signs* that you're healing—even if you're still hurting. These can be small or subtle.

## Messy, Beautiful, Mine: What Healing Looked Like

**Examples:**
- "I no longer feel the need to respond to every message."
- "I made a decision without asking anyone first."
- "I started saying no without a paragraph of explanation."
- "I laughed without guilt."
- "I finally felt... calm."

**Step 2: Write to the You Who Endured**
Write a short letter to the version of you who didn't know how to heal yet. Start with:
*"You were doing your best. Here's what I want you to know now..."*
Speak to that person gently. Let them know what's changed. Let them feel safe. Let them be proud of you.

**Step 3: Choose a Symbol of Healing**
If your healing were an object, what would it be? A key? A cracked bowl? A match? A journal?
- Write why you chose it.
- What does it represent?
- How is your healing showing up in your daily life—through this symbol?

*Healing doesn't ask you to be perfect—it asks you to be honest. And every moment you choose truth over shame, you are healing.*

*I am whole.*

## Chapter 24

# Truth Changes Everything

The truth doesn't just change what you see—it changes how you live. And learning to live with it means giving up the fantasy that kept you stuck—and finally choosing what's real.

I used to cling to hope like it was a lifeline. Hope that he would change. Hope that things would get better. Hope that maybe, just maybe, the version of him I loved would come back. But hope rooted in fantasy isn't hope—it's captivity.

The day I started telling myself the truth, everything shifted. Not all at once. But slowly, my life began to align with what was real—not what I wished was real. I stopped pretending. I stopped performing. I started laughing again. I stopped walking on eggshells in my own home. That's when I realized: the truth wasn't my enemy. It was my freedom.

## Living With the Truth

At some point, the truth stops feeling like a crisis. It becomes less of a shockwave—and more like a steady companion. Not because it stopped mattering, but because you've made room for it inside you. You don't flinch every time it speaks. You don't argue with it. You learn to breathe alongside it.

The truth doesn't disappear. It doesn't rewrite the past or fix everything overnight. But it doesn't destroy you anymore either. Because now, you know how to carry it without letting it carry you away. You know how to stay rooted in what's real—without needing to justify it or explain it to anyone.

## You Stop Arguing with the Past

You stop trying to reframe it. You stop collecting evidence and rewriting the ending in your head. And you stop needing to convince anyone—especially yourself.

The conversations stop replaying. The version where you said the perfect thing, or never said yes in the first place, fades. The story already ended—you don't have to rewrite it anymore.

The questions shift, too. No more asking:

- *"Why didn't I see it?"*
- *"Why did I stay blind so long?"*
- *"How did I let it get that bad?"*

You start answering those questions with something softer:

- *"Because I didn't know what I know now."*
- *"Because I was surviving."*
- *"Because I loved. Because I hoped. Because I tried."*

You stop treating your younger self like a villain in your own story. You start seeing that person as someone who did the best they could with what they had, with what they believed, with what they were taught.

You stop needing to win the argument with your memory. And you start offering it peace. You accept that it happened. That it changed you.

That it broke something *and* built something. And that both can be true at the same time.

## You Don't Forget—But You Don't Live There Anymore

You still remember the details. But they don't hijack you like they used to. You still get triggered sometimes. But you know how to come back to yourself.

You still feel anger, sadness, confusion—But they pass through now. They don't anchor you. You can speak about what happened without shaking. Or sometimes, *you still shake*. But the difference is: you don't apologize for it anymore.

## The Truth Stops Needing to Be Justified

It just is. There's no need for the other person to validate it. No need to explain why you lived that way for so long, or how bad it really was. No need to win the narrative war.

What happened is already known. You know what it cost. You know what it woke up in you. And that's enough.

It's no longer something you carry as a defense. Now, it becomes a boundary.

## You Make Peace with the Person Who Lived It

Not by pretending it was okay. Not by excusing the harm. Not by rewriting history into something cleaner or more heroic. But by telling the truth *all the way through*.

"*Yes, that happened. Yes, I stayed. Yes, I couldn't feel my edges anymore. Yes, I survived. And yes—I'm still becoming more than what was done to me.*"

You stop holding past mistakes like weapons. You stop calling the you who endured weak when it was really exhaustion. You stop criticizing your past choices when it felt like you didn't have any.

You make peace by looking at who you were—with open eyes and an open heart.

You remember how hard you tried. How many times you hoped it would get better. How much you wanted to believe in love, in loyalty, in possibility. How much you gave. How much you gave up.

You start recognizing yourself as someone who was:

- Scared, and stayed anyway.
- Hurting, and kept showing up.
- Isolated, and still found ways to reach for yourself.
- Disappearing, and still carried pieces of hope in your pocket.

**You don't have to admire who you were.**

But you do have to stop abandoning that part of yourself. Because that version of you—the one who kept going—is the reason you made it here. That part kept the light on. And you don't have to erase it to become someone new.

Making peace with the person who lived it isn't weakness. It's strength. It's grace. It's finally returning to what's real.

---

### Self-Check: Are You Still Trying to Prove the Truth?

Living with the truth doesn't mean you forget what happened. It means you stop trying to outrun it, fix it, or make it make sense to people who were never willing to see it.

- You still rehearse the story in your head, trying to find a version where it feels more justified.
- You replay what you *should've said, should've done, should've known*.
- You feel stuck between blaming yourself and blaming them.

- You avoid telling the full truth to others because it still feels overwhelming.
- You still wonder, *"Was it really that bad?"* even though you know it was.
- You find yourself craving validation—just one person to say, *"Yes. That really happened."*
- You keep trying to make meaning out of it before you've fully accepted it.
- You extended forgiveness to them—but haven't yet offered it to yourself.
- You're not sure you trust the version of you who lived through it.
- You're afraid that if you stop thinking about it, it means you're letting them off the hook.

You don't need to justify what you lived through. You only need to believe yourself. That's where peace begins.

## Ways to Reclaim Yourself

You don't need closure to move forward. You just need your own permission to stop fighting what already happened—and start building from what you now know.

- Write down the moment you stopped defending the story.
  Was it a conversation? A realization? A silence that felt too loud?
- Make two lists:
  - "What I used to believe about what happened"
  - "What I know now"

See what shifts. Let the truth settle in.

- Say this out loud or write it in your journal:
  *"It happened. It changed me. It does not define me."*
- Write a letter to the version of yourself who lived through it—not to fix, but to thank. That person got you here.
- Choose one truth you no longer need to explain.

Practice holding it quietly—not as a weapon, not as a wound—but as your own knowing.

You can tell the story with power. You can carry the truth without shame. You can live forward—even with the memory.

## Say It. Write It. Own It.

*You don't have to explain it. You don't have to defend it. Let the light of truth shine through you.*

## Journal Prompt #1:

*What truth have you been carrying like a secret? How would it feel to carry it like a boundary instead?*

## Journal Prompt #2:

*What's something you've spent too long trying to explain, justify, or prove—either to others or to yourself? Are you ready to put it down?*

## Exercise: Let the Truth Be Enough

**Step 1: Write a short, raw version of your story—not the polished version, not the justified one. Just the truth as you lived it.**
Try starting with:
   *"I used to think I was overreacting, but here's what really happened…"*
Don't edit. Don't explain. Just tell the truth for you.

**Step 2: Read it out loud—only to yourself.**
Let your voice hear your own truth.
No disclaimers. No shrinking.

**Step 3: Write one sentence that doesn't need to be defended anymore.**
Let it be the truth you carry forward—quietly, clearly, completely.
   *"I don't need proof. I lived it. And that's enough."*

*Living with the truth doesn't mean
you stay in the pain.
It means you walk in your
power—unapologetically awake.*

*I am transformed.*

# PART IV

# Living Free, Living True

*It's time to stop explaining who you are—and start living like you know.*
*Time to stop shrinking, performing, or asking for permission.*
*You're not here to be palatable. You're here to be real.*

*This is where surviving gives way to living.*
*Where old guilt loosens.*
*Where truth becomes a practice—not just a realization.*

*You're not proving your worth anymore. You're living like you believe it.*
*You'll still shake sometimes. That's okay.*
*But you no longer betray yourself to keep the peace.*
*You feel the fear—and stay with yourself anyway.*
*You're not hiding. You're not waiting. You're not begging to be understood.*
*You're choosing what's true—even when it costs you comfort.*
*You're learning that peace doesn't mean silence—and love doesn't require your suffering.*

I Know Who I Am

*You don't owe anyone your silence to make them comfortable.*
*You don't owe anyone your suffering to prove your love.*

*You are free to be whole.*
*You are allowed to live free.*
*You are ready to live true.*

## Chapter 25

# Staying Isn't Always a Failure. Leaving Isn't Always a Cure

After everything you've faced, the decision to hold on or to walk away isn't always clear. For me, it took years. I believed deeply in marriage, and I tried everything I knew to keep mine alive—prayer, compromise, counseling, sheer endurance. Letting go wasn't quick or easy, and it was never about giving up lightly.

Sometimes, healing begins while you're still inside the story—quietly, invisibly, like a seed cracking open underground. Other times, it starts the moment you step out—when the air hits your lungs differently and you realize you've been holding your breath.

Wherever it begins, there's no universal timeline. No one-size-fits-all moment of clarity. Only the truth of what your heart can hold—and the day you decide your peace is worth protecting.

For me, that moment came when I set a boundary—difficult, yes, but essential if either of us was ever going to heal. I told him I couldn't live that way anymore. Not one more day. I said if he chose to get professional help for his mental health, take his medications, and stop the illegal substances, I would support him. But he looked me in the eye and said, *"That's too hard."*

That was the line. I had given years of effort, but I couldn't make the relationship work alone. I told him he had to leave—that I wouldn't live in that atmosphere for one more minute. He packed his bags and walked out the door.

Your story may look different. Maybe it's a friendship, a family tie, or a job that drains the life out of you. Maybe the choice to remain feels right for now. Maybe the choice to leave comes suddenly. Either way, the moment of truth arrives—the one where your well-being matters more than the illusion of keeping everything together.

## If You Stay, If You Go

People love to ask questions from the outside, as if the answers are simple.

*"Why didn't you leave?"*

*"Why didn't you leave sooner?"*

But they rarely ask the other questions:

*"Why did you stay?"*

*"What did you hope would change?"*

*"What did you risk losing if you walked away—from love, from community, from stability, from the life you'd built?"*

The truth is, these questions don't just belong to marriages. They echo in family ties, friendships, and even work. And the reality is the same: both holding on and stepping away come with a cost. Both are complicated. And both deserve compassion.

## **Staying Isn't Always a Failure. Leaving Isn't Always a Cure.**

People talk like it's simple: Just walk away. Just pack a bag. Just know your worth. But it's not that simple when:

## Staying Isn't Always a Failure. Leaving Isn't Always a Cure

- Your finances are tied to theirs.
- Your children are in the middle.
- Your faith told you to forgive and endure.
- Your family doesn't believe you.
- Your reality has been twisted for so long, you're not sure what's real anymore.
- You depend on the job for survival.
- The person has been a friend for years, and walking away feels like losing history.

Sometimes, you remain because you don't yet have the words for what's happening. Because your nervous system is still frozen. Because you're too tired to move. Because you were taught that endurance is love.

Sometimes, you hold on because you're afraid that walking away will break you—and you're not sure you can come back from that.

And sometimes, you step away. And it hurts more than you thought it would. You don't feel free—you feel shattered. You don't feel strong—you feel wrong. You miss the person who hurt you. You miss the version of yourself who believed it wasn't this bad.

Some people remain for years. Some leave and go back. Some never leave at all. Some create distance quietly and never explain. Some step away in pieces and rebuild in private.

You don't know what someone's carrying until you know:

- What they're afraid of.
- What they're responsible for.
- What they've already survived.
- What stepping away would mean—and what it might break.

Leaving doesn't erase the grief. It doesn't instantly restore your self-worth. It doesn't fix the trauma that's still attached to you.

Remaining isn't weakness. It's often strategy. And sometimes, it's survival. Leaving doesn't mean you're healed. And either way, you're still worthy of care, clarity, and compassion.

You don't owe anyone your story. You don't owe anyone a perfect ending. You only owe yourself the truth—and the freedom to choose from it, again and again.

## Leaving Isn't the End of the Story

It's the beginning of a different kind of grief. Even if it's right. Even if it's necessary. Even if it's life-saving. Because when you leave, you lose more than a person. You lose the version of yourself who kept trying. You lose the hope that maybe this time would be different. You lose the fantasy that love —or loyalty, or faith, or endurance—could fix what hurt you. You may lose a community, a job you depended on, or a friend who carried years of history with you.

Both staying and leaving require grief. Both require strength. Both deserve tenderness.

## What Matters Is That You Stop Abandoning Yourself

Whether you stay or go: You deserve to feel safe in your own mind. You deserve to tell the truth—even if only to yourself. You deserve to set boundaries inside the relationship—or around it. You deserve to protect your peace—even if the world doesn't understand your choices.

This is not about making the "right" decision. It's about no longer leaving yourself behind.

Leaving is one form of liberation. Living in your truth is another. And both count.

If you stay, may you remain awake. If you go, may you walk free. Either way—may you stand fully with yourself.

## It Has to Be Your Choice

You are the one living it. You are the one carrying the consequences—emotionally, physically, financially, spiritually. No one else gets to decide how quickly you wake up, or how long you remain. No one else gets to dictate when you're ready. No one else gets to write the timeline for your freedom.

Leaving can be empowering—but only if it's *your* decision. Staying can be survival—but it doesn't mean you're blind or broken.

You may still be weighing safety. You may still be gathering strength. You may still be grieving what the relationship *could have been.* You may still be waking up from the lie that endurance equals love. All of that is okay.

What matters most isn't what you choose—it's that the choice is yours. Not forced. Not rushed. Not judged.

**Yours.**

## And If You're in Danger...

If you're reading this and wondering, *"Is this just hard—or is it unsafe?"* Please trust that question. Your body knows something. And that knowing deserves your attention.

If you're wondering whether what you're experiencing is "bad enough," let me say this: You don't need bruises to be hurt. You don't need proof to be believed. You don't need permission to protect yourself.

Emotional abuse is real. Manipulation is real. Control, intimidation, isolation – they're real. So is financial control. So is the fear that keeps you silent.

So is the voice in your head asking, *"If I leave, what will happen to me?"* Is your gut whispering, *'this isn't safe;?"* You don't have to wait for it to scream. You are allowed to ask for help before things escalate. You are allowed to plan your safety in quiet ways. You are allowed to leave, even if you can't fully explain why yet.

**This chapter holds space for all kinds of complexity. But if you are in danger—clarity is a gift. And safety is a right.**

I was sitting at my desk, working. My husband was acting strange—stranger than usual. The dogs didn't want him near me. They stayed close, alert. He begged me to come and see something in the garage.

In my gut, I knew I shouldn't go.
I quietly said no.
He pressured. I said no.
He pushed. The dogs got upset.
I said no.
Frustrated, he went upstairs and locked himself in the bedroom.

He had a history of what we called "episodes." He would have dramatic outbursts and manipulative behavior —especially when he felt like he was losing control. Lately, it had been worse. He was unpredictable. Sulking. Constantly making veiled threats.

Later when I left for groceries, I found a noose hanging from the rafters in the garage.

Was it for him—another suicide threat?

Or was it for me?

Why did he want me out there so badly? Why were the dogs so unsettled by his presence?

I wasn't going to find out.

My therapists had already warned me that escalation was likely—that control often tightens before it breaks. He was isolating me—accusing me of things I hadn't done, punishing me with silence and guilt, twisting reality. My therapists gently named what I didn't want to admit yet: gaslighting, control, and emotional manipulation disguised as concern.

I'd seen signs before. But this moment was different. This one felt... final.

That was the moment I knew: **I was in danger.**

If you are in danger, you don't have to be sure to get support. You don't have to have proof to protect yourself. You don't have to be physically harmed to deserve safety.

You are allowed to reach out. You are allowed to plan. You are allowed to leave quietly. You are allowed to prioritize yourself—even if no one else has. You are allowed to protect yourself even when no one else understands.

You are not wrong for wanting to live in peace.

You are not dramatic.

You are not alone.

*If you are in danger, you are not alone. You can call the National Domestic Violence Hotline at 1-800-799-7233 or visit thehotline.org for confidential support. If you are outside the U.S., please look up local hotlines or crisis centers in your area. You deserve safety and peace.*

---

### Self-Check: Are You Still Trying to Earn the Right to Choose?

Staying doesn't make you weak. Leaving doesn't make you selfish. But staying silent with yourself? That's where the real harm lives.

- You've been waiting for it to get worse so you can "justify" leaving.
- You feel like you owe them more chances—even though they've done nothing to change.
- You keep telling yourself *"It's not that bad,"* but your body, mind, and spirit disagree.
- You feel more afraid of the fallout than the relationship itself.
- You can't tell where the guilt ends, and your actual desire begins.
- You second-guess your instincts when you feel anger or dread.
- You fantasize about leaving, but then immediately explain it away.
- You don't feel "allowed" to set boundaries unless you're prepared to walk away.
- You've convinced yourself you need to be completely healed before making a decision.

> - You're waiting for someone else to validate what you already know.
>
> You don't need to be perfect to choose peace. You don't need permission to change your life. You just need to stop abandoning yourself in the name of holding on.

## Ways to Reclaim Yourself

This is not about rushing your decision. This is about waking up in your own life—and starting to listen to what's true for you.

- Write down the story you've been telling yourself about why you have to stay.
  Look at it gently. Whose voice is that? Is it yours—or one you inherited?
- Write another version: *Why you might leave.*
  Not a commitment. Just a truth you're allowed to name.
  Start with: *"If I left, I imagine I would..."*
- Ask yourself this question:
  *"What would I do if I believed I had the right to choose—without guilt, without pressure?"*
- Name the difference between fear and fact.
  Example: *"I'm afraid I'll lose everything."*
  Fact: *"I will lose some things—but maybe I'll gain myself."*
- Choose one way to stop abandoning yourself this week—no matter what decision you make.

Speak the truth. Set a boundary. Ask for help. Rest without apology.
You don't have to know exactly what you want next. You just have to stop pretending this is fine. And that starts now.

## Say It. Write It. Own It.

*It's not about knowing where you're going—it's about no longer pretending where you are.*

## Journal Prompt #1:

*What are the fears, beliefs, or responsibilities that have made leaving feel impossible—or made staying feel necessary? What would it take to hold those with compassion instead of shame?*

## Journal Prompt #2:

*If you could give one piece of advice to a past version of you—the one who was deciding whether to stay or go—what would you say now?*

## Exercise: Write a Permission Slip

### Step 1: Write a short permission slip to yourself.
Let it hold contradictions. Let it hold the messy middle. Let it say what no one ever gave you permission to feel.
Start with:
   *"I'm allowed to…"*

**Examples:**
- "I'm allowed to be unsure."
- "I'm allowed to stay and still want more."
- "I'm allowed to go even if it breaks things."
- "I'm allowed to want peace."
- "I'm allowed to be angry about what I accepted."
- "I'm allowed to change my mind."

**Step 2: Sign your name.**
Because this permission is yours to give now.

*You are not behind. You are not wrong. You are not broken. You are beginning again—with truth, with power, with you..*

*I am free
to choose what's
right for me.*

## Chapter 26

# Triggers, Flashbacks, and Emotional Landmines

Healing doesn't erase what happened. Wherever you are in the process, the most important thing is that healing has begun—even if it's quiet, in the ways you protect yourself, reclaim your body, or just breathe through one more moment.

I remember once seeing a dark car parked down the street from my house. My chest immediately tightened. My heart raced. My shoulders clenched up to my ears. My knees went wobbly, and I felt like I might choke. I was convinced it was him—watching, waiting, stalking me.

It had been years since he left. But my body reacted as if no time had passed at all. I locked myself in the house and closed every blind. Only later did I realize it wasn't him at all—it was my neighbor's daughter, waiting in her car.

It didn't matter. My nervous system had already gone into high alert. That's what trauma does. It teaches your body to brace for danger—even when danger is long gone.

Healing means learning how to feel safe inside yourself again, even when something tries to pull you back in. A smell. A phrase. A memory that shows up uninvited. These aren't signs of failure. They're signs your body is still trying to protect you.

And now, you get to teach it a new story.

## When Technology Keeps You Tethered

An ending doesn't silence fear. It lingers in ordinary moments. The echo shows up in the shape of a parked car, the shadow of a passing face, the sudden buzz of your phone—unexpected and uninvited. What seems harmless to others can feel like a warning to you.

Abuse can continue through technology—long after you've left, blocked, or gone silent. That's not just uncomfortable. It's threatening. It keeps you on edge, never fully free.

You might be experiencing digital abuse if:

- They create fake accounts to view your social media or send messages.
- They use shared devices or apps to track your location without permission.
- They repeatedly text, call, or email—even after you've asked them to stop.
- They demand access to your passwords, messages, or photos.
- They use online platforms to shame, monitor, or control you.
- They threaten to post or share personal content.
- They manipulate mutual connections to send you messages or updates.

You're not imagining things. Being digitally watched, harassed, or followed is real. And it's valid to feel unsafe—even if the threat isn't in the room.

Your safety matters—in every form.

## The Quiet Plans We Made

I found a key in my old wallet the other day. It was small and silver and didn't belong to any place I go now.

It was a key to a friend's house—someone who once looked me in the eye and said, "If you ever need to get out, day or night, just come. Here's a key."

## Triggers, Flashbacks, and Emotional Landmines

She moved away a long time ago. But I never got rid of it. I kept that key not just for the door it opened, but for what it represented: That I had options. That someone believed me. That even if I wasn't ready to leave, I wasn't entirely alone.

I also had a go bag tucked away in a back closet. Not because I planned to use it right then—but because I might need to. I had a mental checklist I ran through every time I felt the tension rising. I knew where my charger was. Where my wallet was. Where the safest exit was.

And in my phone, I had the suicide hotline saved to my favorites. Not for me. For him. Because I was scared of what he might do during one of the downward spirals—when guilt turned into threats and threats turned into pleading and pleading turned into rage. I didn't know how to stop the escalation, but I wanted to have a lifeline ready.

These weren't dramatic gestures. They were quiet ones. Invisible to anyone else—but completely necessary for me to feel like I had some control in a situation that felt anything but safe.

That wasn't paranoia. That was preparation. Survival isn't irrational when the threat is real.

I'm not putting that key in my new wallet I don't need it anymore. Not because I'll never need help again—but because I live differently now. I live without that constant fear. I live in truth. In peace. In choice.

## What was that?

It's been months. Years, even. You're out. You're safe. You're healing. And then, out of nowhere— a phrase. A look. A certain silence. A smell. An off-hand comment. And suddenly, you're *right back there.*

Your chest tightens. Your breath shortens. Your hands are shaking. Your heart is racing. You can't think straight. You feel yourself spiraling. You feel ashamed for overreacting—but it doesn't *feel* like an overreaction. You wonder: *What's wrong with me? Why am I still reacting like this?*

That's a flashback.

But here's the truth:

Nothing is wrong with you. Something happened to you—and your body still remembers.

## Flashbacks Aren't Just Visual—They're Emotional

We often picture flashbacks as vivid images playing in someone's mind, like a movie reel of the past. And yes, sometimes it's that. But for many survivors, flashbacks don't come with pictures. Sometimes you see it. But often, you just *feel* it:

- The sudden terror in your chest
- The panic without cause
- The deep freeze when someone raises their voice
- The collapse when someone withdraws affection
- The urge to run, shut down, explode, disappear

You might not remember the moment that caused it. You might not see anything. But inside? Your body is *screaming*. And it's doing what it was trained to do: **react, protect, survive.**

That's not imagination. That's memory.

And it makes sense: when you didn't feel safe in the past, your body learned to stay alert. Even after years of setting boundaries and making choices for your own healing, your nervous system still keeps watch always scanning for danger. Because for a long time, you weren't overreacting. You were under protected.

## Triggers Aren't Drama. They're Data.

It's easy to feel ashamed when you're triggered. You might think, *"It's been so long, I should be past this."* Or worse, *"I'm being too emotional."*

But triggers are not tantrums. They're not weakness. They're not signs that you're broken. They're not evidence that you're failing. They're reminders that something hurt—and your body remembers. They're your nervous system's alarm bells—sometimes ringing too loud, too early, but always with a reason.

A trigger is simply something that awakens a pain point you didn't know was still tender. You're being pulled into an old emotional state by a present-day reminder. It's not about what's happening now—it's about what it reminds your body of.

Triggers show you:

- You're triggered when you feel hurt and unsafe.
- You're triggered when you run across something that feels unfinished or ungrieved.
- You're triggered when part of you still doesn't feel protected.
- You're triggered when someone gives you the same silent treatment your partner used to.
- You're triggered when a friend's sarcasm sounds like a familiar cruelty.
- You're triggered when a tone, gesture, or word sends your body into high alert.

That doesn't make you fragile. It means you've been impacted. And your body is doing its best to keep you safe—sometimes even when safety is already here.

## The Goal Isn't to Never Be Triggered—It's to Know What to Do When You Are

This isn't about being calm all the time. You don't have to live in fear of your own emotions. The goal isn't to erase every trigger—it's to build the capacity to respond instead of react.

It's about building awareness:

- *What sets me off?*
- *What does it feel like in my body?*

- *What story am I telling myself right now?*
- *What's true—and what's leftover fear?*
- *What does my body need to feel safe again?*

You begin to notice:

- *This feels like then, but it's not then.*
- *This person isn't that person.*
- *I can pause, I can breathe, I can stay.*

You can't always stop the flashback. But you can stop the shame spiral that follows. Getting triggered doesn't mean you're failing—it means your body is remembering. And now, you get to remember, too: you don't have to disappear anymore.

You can learn to feel it—without believing it.

## What Healing Looks Like Now

Healing doesn't mean you never get scared. It means you know what to do when fear shows up. You get to remind yourself that this time—you're the one in charge.

You start noticing the signs earlier.

You hold your breath for a moment—then exhale.

Your body tightens—but you stay with yourself instead of abandoning your needs.

You pause instead of reacting. You give yourself options.

You don't spiral—you ground.

You don't lash out—you listen.

You talk to yourself the way you wish someone had talked to you when you were small and scared.

You don't flee—you stay. Not in harm's way—but in your own body.

And when you can't? When the panic wins or the flashback takes over? You show yourself grace. Because even that is part of healing.

The body remembers. But now, so do you. And this time, you're safe.

## Self-Check: Are You Still Reacting to a Past That Feels Like the Present?

Flashbacks and triggers don't mean you're broken. They mean your body still remembers what it was like to feel small, unsafe, or unheard. And healing means learning to listen—without fear.

- You react strongly to small things and then feel ashamed afterward.
- You feel flooded by emotion without knowing why.
- You often think *"I know this isn't a big deal, but it feels huge."*
- You freeze when you need to speak up—or say something and then panic.
- You replay conversations obsessively, trying to figure out what went wrong.
- You feel anxious or edgy in safe environments, like you're waiting for something bad to happen.
- You've told yourself *"I should be over this by now."*
- You feel like your emotions don't match the moment—and it makes you question your sanity.
- You blame yourself for "ruining good things" when your fear takes over.
- You struggle to trust people who haven't done anything wrong—because your body still expects them to.

This isn't about being irrational. It's about being injured—and learning how to heal with care instead of criticism.

## Ways to Reclaim Yourself

You don't have to be fearless. You just have to stop abandoning yourself when fear shows up.

- Notice the next time you feel "off" without an obvious reason. Don't rush to fix it. Just pause and ask:
  *"What does this remind me of?"*
  *"Where do I feel this in my body?"*
- Keep a "Trigger Map" journal.
  Jot down moments when your reactions felt bigger than the moment. Look for patterns—not to shame yourself, but to build awareness.
- When a flashback hits, ground yourself with the five senses:
  *What can I see? Hear? Touch? Smell? Taste?*
  *What is true right now? What's not happening anymore?*
- Learn to say to yourself, softly and clearly:
  *"I'm safe now.*
  *I'm not there anymore.*
  *I can take care of myself this time."*
- Give your body what it needs—not what you were taught to deny. Rest. Movement. Boundaries. Stillness. Support.
  You don't have to explain your need for calm.

*You don't have to control every reaction.*
*You just need to meet yourself there—with truth and tenderness.*

## Say It. Write It. Own It.

*Even in the dark, you can hold the light of your own truth. You're not lost—you're finding your way back to yourself.*

## Journal Prompt #1:

*When was the last time you were triggered and didn't understand why at first? Looking back, what do you think your body was trying to tell you?*

## Journal Prompt #2:

*What do you tend to say to yourself when you feel anxious, flooded, or overwhelmed? What would it feel like to respond with kindness instead of criticism?*

## Exercise: Create a Grounding Script

### Step 1: Write a simple grounding phrase you can return to in the moment.

Use your own words or start with one of these:
- *"This feels like then, but it's not then."*
- *"I'm safe now. I can stay with myself."*
- *"This fear is real—but so is my strength."*

### Step 2: Add sensory grounding tools.

Choose 1–2 grounding actions that work for you:
- Touch something with texture (a stone, a blanket, a piece of jewelry).
- Run cold water over your hands.
- Smell a calming scent (lavender, peppermint, etc.).
- Name five things you can see, four you can touch, three you can hear, two you can smell, one you can taste.

**Step 3: Practice it when you're not triggered.**
Say it out loud, write it on a card, or keep it in your journal. Build the habit gently so it feels accessible when you need it most.

*There will still be moments that*
*bring fear—make you shake, cause you to flinch.*
*But now, you meet them with truth—and*
*no longer give them the power to shape who you are.*

*I am light—steady, strong, and sure.*

## INTERLUDE

# What Real Love Looks Like

### A Glimpse of Real Love

It doesn't start with fireworks. It starts with peace. Not performance. Not pressure. Not pain you learn to reinterpret as passion.

Real love feels steady. Safe. Quiet, even—at least at first. Because your nervous system doesn't have to brace. Your heart doesn't have to bargain. You don't have to explain your wounds before you're treated with care.

**Real Love Doesn't Feel Like Something You Have to Prove.**

You don't have to earn your place. You don't have to shrink to fit their expectations. You don't have to manage their moods just to feel okay in the room. Real love doesn't require you to forget yourself.

You get to say what you want. You get to name what hurt. You get to have needs—and still feel safe. And when you mess up, you're not made to pay for it with silence or shame.

You talk.

You listen.

You stay human—together.

## Real Love Isn't Perfect. It's Respectful.

It doesn't mean they'll never annoy you. It doesn't mean you won't have to work. It doesn't mean there won't be growth, tension, repair. But it means you're not alone in the effort. You're not the only one reaching. And love isn't something you're afraid to lose every time you speak up.

Real love doesn't walk away when you're hard to hold. It leans in—with gentleness, not control.

## What Real Love Sounds Like

**Real love** doesn't just show up in action. It shows up in words—the kind that hold, not harm.
*"You don't have to fix it. I'm here."*
**Real love** doesn't rush you out of your pain. It sits beside you in it.
You're not a burden —and you're not a problem to be solved.
You are allowed to feel without apologizing for it.
*"I believe you."*
**Real love** doesn't question your story.
It doesn't need proof, performance, or explanation.
It listens—and trusts the truth you've lived.
*"That makes sense."*
**Real love** connects the dots with you.
It doesn't make you feel irrational, dramatic, or broken for reacting.
It validates your experience before it offers advice.
*"Tell me more."*
**Real love** is curious.
Not suspicious. Not defensive.
It wants to understand—not control the narrative.
*"You're not too much."*
**Real love** makes space for all of you.
The big feelings. The complexity. The honesty.

## What Real Love Looks Like

You don't have to water yourself down to be loved.
*"You can say no and I'll still be here."*
**Real love** respects boundaries.
It doesn't punish you for having limits.
It honors your "no" just as deeply as it welcomes your "yes."
*"I care about how you feel."*
**Real love** doesn't just want things to look good.
It wants you to *be okay.*
Your emotional reality matters—and it's not dismissed or minimized.
*"I'm not going anywhere."*
**Real love** doesn't make you earn consistency.
It's not conditional on performance or perfection.
It stays—not to trap you, but to build safety over time.

*Real love isn't earned.*
*It's not fragile.*
*It doesn't silence your truth to preserve the connection.*
*It includes your truth—and makes room for your whole self.*
*Love is very patient and kind,*
*It's never jealous or envious,*
*Love is never boastful or proud,*
*It's never haughty or selfish or rude.*
*It never behaves inappropriately.*
*Love puts you first.*
*Love does not demand its own way.*
*It's not irritable or touchy.*
*Love doesn't keep score.*
*Love does not hold grudges.*
*It's never glad about injustice.*
*Love celebrates whenever truth wins out.*
*When someone loves you, they will be loyal to you no matter what the cost.*
*They will believe in you,*

I Know Who I Am

*They will expect the best for you.*
*They will stand their ground defending you.*
*Because you are worth it.*

And when you finally feel it—you'll know. Not because it demands anything, but because it lets you be exactly who you are.

*I am worthy
of real love.*

## CHAPTER 27

## I Know Who I Am

I was sitting at the table with the radio playing—a small thing, but it felt like a shift. For years, I hadn't listened to music. Not the kind I liked. Not the kind that made me feel. But that day, a rhythm came through the speakers and something inside me stirred. I started tapping my toes. Then I stood up. And I danced. Just me, the music, and a pair of dogs losing their minds in delight. I laughed out loud—real, full, joyful laughter. I had loved dancing once. And I had forgotten. But in that moment, I remembered.

There's a moment when you realize you're not surviving anymore. You're choosing. You're speaking. You're living. And for the first time—you know exactly who you are.

### Coming Home to Yourself

There's a quiet moment—sometimes unexpected—when you realize you've returned to yourself. It doesn't come with fanfare. It doesn't always feel triumphant. Sometimes, it arrives while you're folding laundry, or walking alone, or standing in the shower letting the water wash over skin that has survived too much. And suddenly, something inside you whispers:

*I know who I am.*

Not who you were taught to be. Not who you had to become to stay safe. Not who you pretended to be to avoid punishment. Not who you became to feel lovable. Not who you performed to keep the peace.

You find yourself again slowly —like light seeping through a crack in a long-closed door you thought would never open. You find that your voice doesn't tremble as much. Your "yes" and your "no" begin to carry weight. Your body, once a battleground of tension and hiding, begins to feel like shelter.

And it's not because everything is perfect now. It's because something in you decided—no more. No more shrinking. No more explaining your worth. No more twisting yourself into knots to be palatable or pleasing.

This chapter is not just a conclusion. It's a reclamation.

This is the part where you stop asking for permission to exist. Where you stop waiting for someone else to define you. This is where you take your life, gently but firmly, back into your own hands.

Because now, you know.

## Who I Used to Be

I used to think love was something I had to earn. I used to think if I could just be good enough—calm enough, forgiving enough, needed enough— then maybe they would finally see me. Maybe they would treat me better. Maybe I could stop hurting.

I confused love with survival. I mistook caretaking for connection. I called it loyalty when really, it was fear. I didn't know that disappearing for someone else isn't the same thing as being close to them. I didn't know how much of myself I was giving up just to keep the peace.

Back then, I didn't understand that constantly second-guessing myself wasn't a personal flaw—it was a symptom of manipulation. I didn't know that walking on eggshells wasn't normal. I didn't know that the dread I felt before a conversation, the way I flinched at silence, the exhaustion I carried every day—those were signs I was surviving, not living.

I made myself small. I apologized for things that weren't my fault. I tried to be perfect. I stayed quiet when I wanted to scream. I accepted crumbs and convinced myself I was full. But here's the thing: I loved the person I used to be.

I did the best I could with what I had. I was brave, even when I was scared. I kept showing up, even when it hurt. I was trying to make something work—even though it was destroying me.. I didn't fail. I adapted. I endured. I survived.

And I honor the me who endured—not as a warning, but as a warrior. That version of me carried me here.

## Who I Am Now

I am no longer willing to lose myself to keep someone else. I know the sound of my own voice now. I trust it and I trust myself. I don't need someone else to validate my worth or shape my identity. I know how to stand still in my truth, even if it makes other people uncomfortable.

I know what peace feels like. I used to chase intensity, thinking it was love—but now I recognize the difference. I know the quiet, steady hum of safety. I know what it's like to speak without fear. To rest without guilt. To choose without asking permission.

I don't chase people anymore. I don't explain myself to those committed to misunderstanding me. I don't try to manage how others see me, because I finally see *myself*—clearly, fully, and with compassion.

I know what love is supposed to feel like. And I know now that love isn't supposed to hurt. It doesn't have to be earned. It doesn't demand your silence, or your suffering, or your soul.

I have boundaries—not walls, not punishments, but loving, firm reminders that I matter too. I can say "no" and still be kind. I can walk away and still be whole.

I am growing and healing—but that doesn't make me broken. That makes me alive. I am not who I was before. I am not who they tried to make me. I am not who I pretended to be just to survive. I am who I choose to be now.

And that choice is mine.

## What I No Longer Accept

There are things I used to tolerate because I thought I had to. Because I didn't know I had choices. Because I was scared of what would happen if I stood up, spoke out, or walked away. Not anymore.

I refuse to be blamed for someone else's behavior. I no longer accept gaslighting, manipulation, or the slow erosion of my confidence disguised as "love." I do not accept conditional affection—the kind that only shows up when I'm silent, small, or serving.

I no longer accept relationships where I have to earn the right to feel safe. I don't accept being punished—for having needs, for being human, for simply existing. I refuse to carry all the emotional weight as the price of being close to someone. I will not carry pain that isn't mine anymore. I reject the lie that I am unacceptable or not enough. I no longer contort myself to fit someone else's comfort zone.

What I accept now is respect. Reciprocity. Accountability. Softness. Laughter. Freedom. Space to breathe and be.

And if someone can't offer that? I would rather embrace their absence than accept their disrespect and harm.

## What I'm Still Learning

Healing isn't a finish line. It's a path I walk every day. I am still learning how to trust my own nervous system—how to tell the difference between intuition and fear, between discomfort and danger. Sometimes I still flinch at kindness and second-guess peace, because for a long time, chaos was home.

I am learning that I don't have to earn rest. That I can receive love without suspicion. That I don't have to apologize for needing space, or asking questions, or saying "no." I am learning how to live in a body I used to ignore or punish. How to listen when it whispers instead of waiting until it screams. I am learning how to celebrate without waiting for the other shoe to drop. How to accept joy without guilt. How to be proud of myself without shrinking.

I am still unlearning the lies that were handed to me: that I was hard to love, that I was too emotional, too needy, too sensitive, too demanding, too perfect. I am learning that all of those things were *never* flaws. They were signals. They were evidence of my depth and my truth and my humanity.

I am learning how to be in relationships where I don't disappear. I am learning how to be alone without being lonely. How to belong to myself first. How to create safety from the inside out.

And maybe most of all, I'm learning that it's okay to not have it all figured out. Healing is not a performance. Growth is not a straight line. I can stumble. I can take breaks. I can come back to myself as many times as I need to.

That, too, is strength—the courage to live as the fullest version of yourself, the freedom to keep growing into who you were always meant to be, and the audacity to turn survival into unapologetic living.

### Self-Check: Are You Letting Yourself Take Up Space in Your Own Life?

This chapter marks a new step in your growth—a decision to keep moving forward into your truest self. Sometimes, even after we've made the choice to move forward, old habits linger. Use this self-check to notice where you may still be shrinking, doubting, or waiting for permission to be who you are.

- You still catch yourself apologizing for things that aren't your fault.

- You struggle to make decisions without checking how others will feel about them.
- You hesitate to celebrate your growth because you're afraid of being judged or drawing attention.
- You sometimes downplay your needs—even when you know they're valid.
- You feel guilty for resting, slowing down, or choosing peace over productivity.
- You worry that your wholeness might cost you connection.
- You wonder if claiming your power means you're being selfish or cold.
- You fear outgrowing people you once needed to survive.
- You sometimes second-guess your healing when someone challenges your boundaries.
- You still wait for external validation—even when your inner truth is clear.

You don't have to fix all of this overnight. But you *can* begin noticing. And honoring. And choosing differently.

## Ways to Reclaim Yourself

You are already on the path. Now, it's about deepening your roots in your own truth—living like you belong to yourself.

- **Let your "no" be complete.** No explanation. No softening. No second-guessing.

# I Know Who I Am

- **Celebrate something small.** Not to prove anything—just because it's yours to be proud of.
- **Unfollow, mute, or release the voices that pull you back into self-doubt.**
- **Return to your grounding rituals.** The music, scents, textures, or movements that remind you who you are.
- **Speak your truth in a space where it will be honored**—*or* write it where no one else can touch it.
- **Practice choosing without apologizing.** Start with something small. Choose it for *you*.
- **Say it aloud: "I know who I am."** Say it again when you feel shaky. Say it again when you don't believe it yet.
- **Trust the version of you that no longer flinches at your own power.**

You don't have to prove that you're healed to begin living like you're whole.

You are allowed to belong to yourself now.

## Say It. Write It. Own It.

*Even now, you are worthy of your own truth. You don't have to wait for someone else to see it. You know who you are—and you get to live like it.*

## Journal Prompt #1:

*What does self-trust look like for me right now?*

I Know Who I Am

*How do I know when I'm honoring my truth?*

## Journal Prompt #2:

*Where in my life do I feel most aligned with who I truly am?*
*What choices have helped me feel that way?*

## Journal Prompt #3:

*What part of me still needs reassurance that I am safe, worthy, and allowed to take up space?*
*What would I say to that part?*

## Exercise: Remembering Who You Are

*You don't owe anyone the smaller version of you. You get to be free—even when it's new, even when it's still unfolding.*

## A Guided Practice

Find a quiet moment. Sit comfortably. Take a slow breath in, and as you exhale, feel yourself settle deeper into your body.

Now imagine this:

You're standing at the edge of a forest. Behind you is the road you've walked—long, winding, sometimes brutal. You glance back and nod. Not with regret, but with recognition. You honor the version of you who kept going.

In front of you is a clearing, open and sunlit. The path ahead is yours to choose. No one is pulling the strings. No one else gets to tell your story from here. You feel the ground beneath your feet—solid, certain.

Breathe into that truth. And now, repeat softly—or write, or speak aloud—these words:

I AM
*I am whole, even as I heal.*
*I am allowed to take up space.*
*I am not what happened to me.*
*I am not here to be anyone's version of acceptable.*
*I am free to change.*
*I am deserving of love that feels like peace.*
*I am becoming someone I can trust.*
*I am enough—not because I'm perfect, but because I am real.*
*I am already worthy. I always was.*

Now, gently return to the present moment. If you'd like, write a short letter to the version of yourself who doubted this day would ever come. You might begin like this:

> *Dear me,*
> *You don't have to carry it all anymore. You don't have to earn your own love. I see you now—the way you kept going, the way you protected your hope even when you were hurting. Thank you for surviving. Thank you for not giving up. I promise to stay with you now. I know who you are. And you are safe with me.*

## Guided Journaling: I Know Who I Am

Take your time. These questions aren't a test—they're an invitation. You don't have to answer them all at once. Let your truth come gently. Let your story rise without shame.

Use these prompts to reflect, release, and reconnect with who you truly are.

### 1. Looking Back with Clarity

What version of me did I create to survive?
What was I taught to believe about love, worth, or identity that I now question?
What parts of me did I hide or shrink to be "enough" for someone else?

### 2. Naming My Growth

What's something I've done recently that past-me would be proud of?
How do I speak to myself now, compared to before?
What am I doing today that reflects the fact that I *know who I am*?

### 3. Letting Go with Intention

What am I no longer willing to carry?
Whose voice do I need to quiet in order to hear my own?
What belief, habit, or pattern am I ready to release—gently, but firmly?

### 4. Reclaiming My Voice

Finish this sentence as many times as you need to:
**"I am not..."** (e.g., I am not too sensitive. I am not broken. I am not a burden.)
Now finish this one:
**"I am..."** (e.g., I am enough. I am powerful. I am learning. I am mine.)

## 5. Calling Myself Home

If I could write one promise to myself and mean it, it would be:
**"I promise…"**
If I could say one thing to the version of me who doubted I'd ever feel whole, it would be:
**"Dear me…"**

*Let this page be sacred. Let it be messy.*
*Let it be yours.*
*You're not becoming someone else.*
*You're becoming yourself—on purpose,*
*with love, and without apology.*

*I know who I am,
and I count that as
victory.*

# Stepping Into Your New Tomorrow Your New Beginning

This is not the end. It's the beginning. You've shed the skin of survival. You've faced truths you once couldn't bear to name. You've stood in the wreckage and decided to rebuild—this time, with *you* at the center.

You no longer have to beg for love that costs you your peace. You no longer have to explain your worth to people who refuse to see it. You don't have to become someone else to be safe. You're not who they told you that you were. You are who you *chose* to become.

This new tomorrow doesn't promise perfection. It promises possibility. It gives you room to breathe, to rest, to stumble —and still rise. It makes space for your joy, your softness, your boundaries, your voice.

Now, you love differently—because you love from a place of wholeness. You listen to your body. You honor your truth.

You leave when you're ready. You stay when staying feels safe, or necessary, or not yet ready. Either way, your experience is valid. You no longer abandon yourself to be chosen by someone else.

You don't need anyone's permission to begin again. You're already doing it.

There will still be hard days. There will still be moments when you forget. But now you have a map. A compass. A voice. A self. And you can always begin again tomorrow.

So, step forward—not as a version of who you were, but as the person you've fought to become.

## I Know Who I Am

You're not who you used to be. You're not who they wanted you to be. You're *you*.

And tomorrow?

It belongs to you now.

Because now —without question, without apology, without fear, you know.

**I know who I am.**

And that changes everything.

# Letter to Myself

You've made it to the end of the book—but not the end of your story.

This is a letter for the version of you who made it here. The one who kept going. The one who's learning to trust themself again.

You don't have to rewrite the past—you've already done that work.

Now is your chance to speak to the you who exists today. The one who has lived this truth. The one who is choosing healing, one breath at a time.

What do you want to carry forward? What do you want to remember the next time doubt whispers or fear returns?

What do you want to promise yourself now?

Write it here. You don't have to get it perfect. Just get it honest.

This is your page. No edits. No filters. Just you.

# Next Steps

*You don't have to know what's next to take the next step.*

You've done something courageous: you told yourself the truth. You stayed with your story. You chose to see clearly—and that's the beginning of everything.

There's no finish line for healing, no checklist for becoming whole. But if you're wondering what now, here are a few things to remember:

- You can come back to these pages anytime. Healing isn't linear. Repetition is not failure.

- You can keep writing. Keep noticing. Keep choosing yourself in small, everyday ways.

- You don't have to do it alone. Reach out. Let yourself be witnessed by people who feel safe, not just familiar.

- You get to define what peace means now. What home feels like in your body. What love should never ask you to sacrifice.

- You're already doing the hardest part: staying present with yourself.

- Whatever you do next, let it be kind. Let it be yours.

# A Note from Me to You

If you made it here—page by page, truth by truth—I want you to know something:

This may be the end of the book but it's the beginning of what comes next. And I want to thank you.

Thank you for showing up. For staying with your story, even when it hurt. For being willing to tell yourself the truth—and let go of what was never yours to carry.

I see you. I honor your courage. And I'm proud of you.

Writing this book meant returning to some of the hardest places I've been. I didn't do it to live the pain again—I did it so you wouldn't have to walk through yours alone. If reading these words helped you feel even a little more seen, more whole, more yourself —then it was worth every page. We are meant to witness and be witnessed. To walk beside each other, reminding one another of who we really are.

This book wasn't about fixing you. You were never broken.

It's not about becoming perfect. It never was.
It's about becoming you —on purpose.

## I Know Who I Am

It's about remembering who you are—and giving yourself permission to be that, unapologetically.

It's about learning to trust your own voice and take up space without apology.
It's about choosing love that doesn't require you to disappear.

Keep going. Keep choosing you.
You don't need permission to begin again.
You already have everything you need inside you.

So, take this next step —boldly, gently, bravely. Whatever way feels true.
This is your new tomorrow. And I believe in it.
I believe in you.

All my heart,
Pamela

# Acknowledgements

This book almost didn't happen.

There were years I couldn't speak the truth—let alone write it. But I'm here now. And that's because I wasn't alone.

To my family and friends who never asked me to shrink, thank you for seeing the real me before I could.
To those who encouraged this book when it was only a whisper—thank you for reminding me that my story matters.
To the ones who prayed, checked in, sent quiet encouragement—you'll never know how much it meant.

To my dearest friends (you know who you are)—thank you for standing with me through every tear, every breakdown, and every breakthrough. Your presence was a lifeline.

Thank you to my children and grandchildren, who keep showing me what love without fear looks like. You are the brightest parts of my story.

And to the reader holding this book—you are why I wrote it. If you saw yourself in these pages, I hope you also saw your strength, your voice, and your freedom.

I know who I am.

And I see you.

# Pamela D. White

Pamela D. White is a survivor, teacher, and the author of more than a dozen published books.

After surviving emotional abuse that left her questioning her worth, she began the long work of reclaiming her voice and trusting herself again. *I Know Who I Am* is her most personal work to date—a survivor's guide written for those who stayed quiet, made themselves small, and kept surviving anyway.

Pam holds degrees in Education and Organizational Leadership and spent nearly twenty years in the classroom before shifting her focus to writing, mentoring, and helping others tell the truth about their stories. She lives in the prairie land of central Illinois, where she walks with her dogs, laughs with her grandchildren, and reconnects with the friends who always saw her clearly.

# Before the Glossary

## A Note About the Words

You don't need to know every term in this glossary to understand your story—but sometimes, having the right words helps you name what you've been through.

This isn't here to diagnose you. It's here to support you. To remind you that the confusion wasn't your fault. That what happened had a name. That what you're building now—healing, truth, self-trust—has names too.

Read what you need. Leave the rest. Come back when it helps.

# Glossary of Terms

*A gentle guide to words that describe the harm, the healing, and the truth.*

##  Core Definitions

### Abuse
Any repeated behavior used to dominate, control, shame, or harm another person—physically, emotionally, sexually, financially, or psychologically. Abuse isn't just about anger or violence. It's about power. If someone consistently makes you feel small, afraid, confused, or unworthy—you're not too sensitive. That's abuse.

### Emotional Abuse
A pattern of words, actions, or silence used to control, belittle, confuse, or intimidate someone. It can include criticism, gaslighting, stonewalling, guilt-tripping, threats, or constant blame. Emotional abuse doesn't leave bruises, but it leaves deep scars.

### Trauma Bond
An intense, confusing attachment that forms in a cycle of abuse—where moments of kindness, guilt, or intimacy are used to keep you hooked after harm. You may feel loyal, responsible, or even dependent on someone who hurts you. That doesn't mean you're weak—it means your nervous system is doing its best to survive something painful.

##  Abuse + Control Tactics

### Gaslighting
A form of manipulation where someone causes you to doubt your own memory, perception, or reality. It often sounds like "That never happened" or "You're overreacting."

**Love Bombing**
Excessive praise, attention, or gifts used early in a relationship to create dependency, often followed by devaluation or withdrawal.

**Coercive Control**
A pattern of controlling behaviors—like isolating someone, monitoring their movements, or making them feel guilty—that limit a person's freedom or sense of safety.

**Manipulation**
A tactic used to control or influence someone—often by twisting facts, using guilt, withholding affection, or playing on fears. It can feel confusing because it's often subtle, disguised as concern, love, or logic.

**Psychological Punishment**
Subtle or overt tactics used to cause emotional pain, guilt, or fear when someone doesn't comply. This can include silent treatment, guilt trips, emotional withdrawal, threats, or shame.

**Traumatic Tactics**
Behaviors that cause emotional shock, fear, or confusion—like verbal abuse, gaslighting, or explosive anger. They create a climate of unpredictability that keeps you on edge.

**Silent Treatment**
Withholding communication, affection, or attention as a form of punishment or control. It creates fear, shame, and emotional instability.

**Narcissistic Behavior**
Patterns marked by entitlement, lack of empathy, and a need for control or admiration. Not everyone with these traits has a diagnosis, but the impact on others can still be deeply harmful.

**Isolation**
A tactic used to cut you off from friends, family, or support—often disguised as concern, jealousy, or "us against the world." It makes it harder to ask for help or see the truth clearly.

**Guilt-Tripping**
Using shame, obligation, or emotional pressure to make you feel bad for setting boundaries, expressing needs, or saying no.

**Victim-Playing**
When someone harms you but then paints themselves as the one who's been wronged—often to avoid accountability or gain sympathy.

**Hoovering**
A tactic used to "suck" you back in after you've pulled away. It may involve fake apologies, love bombing, sudden crises, or promises of change.

**Breadcrumbing**
Giving just enough affection, attention, or hope to keep you attached—but never enough to create emotional safety or growth.

**Projection**
Blaming you for things they are doing themselves—like accusing you of lying or overreacting to deflect attention from their own behavior.

**Smear Campaign**
A calculated effort to damage your reputation—often through lies, half-truths, or manipulation of mutual relationships.

**Overprotecting**
An emotionally abusive tactic where one person excessively controls or restricts another's actions under the guise of care or concern. It often leads to isolation, fear, and a loss of autonomy—masking control as "protection."

**Body Shaming**
Criticizing or mocking someone's appearance—weight, facial features, clothing, or body type—to assert control or superiority. Sometimes disguised as "jokes" or "concern," it chips away at confidence and reinforces power imbalances.

**Damaging Property**
Destroying or harming objects—walls, doors, dishes, or personal belongings—to intimidate, threaten, or assert control. Even if the harm isn't directed at a person, it sends a loud message: *Look what I'm capable of.*

**Sleep Deprivation**
Deliberately disrupting someone's ability to rest or sleep—through noise, light, arguments, or forced routines. Chronic sleep disruption weakens emotional resilience and makes it harder to think clearly or maintain boundaries.

**Name-Calling**
Using insults, labels, or sarcastic "compliments" to degrade, belittle, or manipulate. It can sound cruel ("You're worthless") or disguised as a jab ("You think you're so perfect"), but its impact is the same: to undermine your self-worth.

**Stalking**
Monitoring your movements, following you without consent, or showing up uninvited. Stalking is a form of control that creates fear and instability, often masked as "concern" but driven by obsession, jealousy, or intimidation.

##  Trauma + Nervous System

**Survival Mode**
A physical and emotional state where your body and mind are focused on staying safe—often at the cost of rest, clarity, or connection. It's not weakness—it's adaptation.

### Fight, Flight, Freeze, Fawn

Common trauma responses:
- **Fight**: Defending or confronting.
- **Flight**: Escaping or avoiding.
- **Freeze**: Numbing or shutting down.
- **Fawn**: People-pleasing or over-accommodating to stay safe.

### Trigger

A sensory, emotional, or situational cue that activates a trauma response—often without warning.

### Flashback

A sudden re-experiencing of a past traumatic moment. It may be emotional, visual, or physical—even if the danger is no longer present.

## Healing + Reclamation

### Boundaries

Limits you set to protect your well-being—emotionally, physically, spiritually, or mentally. Healthy boundaries are a sign of self-respect.

### Self-Abandonment

Ignoring or dismissing your own needs, emotions, or truth in order to keep others comfortable or maintain peace.

### Self-Trust

The ability to believe your own feelings, needs, and instincts—even when others doubt or dismiss them.

### Emotional Safety

The feeling of being accepted, heard, and respected in a relationship. You don't have to walk on eggshells or fear emotional backlash for being yourself.

**Reclamation**
The ongoing process of returning to your own voice, worth, and power—especially after being made to feel small or unworthy.

**Empowerment**
Reconnecting with your own choices and voice. It's not about becoming someone new—it's about remembering who you were before the fear.

**Reparenting**
Caring for yourself the way you may not have been cared for—through protection, consistency, comfort, and love.

**Grounding**
Practices that help bring you back to the present moment when you feel overwhelmed or disconnected. Grounding reminds your body that it's safe to come home.

**Self-Compassion**
Offering yourself the same kindness and patience you would give someone you love. It softens shame, blame, and perfectionism.

**Integration**
Making peace with your story—not by forgetting it, but by weaving it into who you are with honesty and gentleness. Integration turns survival into self-ownership.

# Resources

Healing is a journey—and sometimes, we need extra support. Here are resources that may help you on your path:

## Books & Workbooks

- *Codependent No More by Melody Beattie*
- *The Language of Letting Go: Daily Meditations for Codependents by Melody Beattle*
- *Stop Walking on Eggshells by Paul T. Mason and Randi Kreger*
- *Boundaries by Dr. Henry Cloud and Dr. John Townsend*
- *Good Boundaries and Goodbyes: Loving Others Without Losing the Best of Who You Are by Lysa TerKeurst*
- *Shifting from brokenness to wholeness.: Making Art- Makes Sense by Martina Keast*
- *Healing the Soul of a Woman by Joyce Meyer*
- *Beauty for Ashes by Joyce Meyer*

## Support Networks

- Local counseling and therapy services
- Support groups for survivors of emotional abuse (online and in person)
- Trusted friends, mentors, or spiritual advisors

## Helplines & Emergency Support

- **National Domestic Violence Hotline:** 1-800-799-7233
  www.thehotline.org

- **National Network to End Domestic Violence (NNEDV) Safety Net Project**
  Offers practical guidance for survivors experiencing technology-based abuse, including cyberstalking, digital harassment, GPS tracking, and phone monitoring. Learn how to protect your devices, secure your accounts, and stay safer in a digital world.
  https://www.techsafety.org
- **Suicide & Crisis Lifeline (U.S.):** 988
  Available 24/7 for anyone in emotional distress or suicidal crisis.
  www.988lifeline.org
- **Crisis Text Line:** Text HOME to 741741
  www.crisistextline.org
- **Substance Abuse and Mental Health Services Administration (SAMHSA) National Helpline:**
  1–800–662–HELP (4357)
  Free and confidential help for mental health or substance use concerns.
  www.samhsa.gov/find-help/national-helpline
- **Local emergency services:** 911 or your country's equivalent

## Online Resources & Communities

- **RAINN (Rape, Abuse & Incest National Network)**
  www.rainn.org — Support for survivors of sexual violence, including live chat and hotline.
- **Psych Central Forums**
  forums.psychcentral.com — Peer-support forums for emotional health and recovery.
- **The Mighty**
  www.themighty.com — A community of people sharing lived experiences with trauma, mental health, and resilience.

- **Therapy for Black Girls**
  www.therapyforblackgirls.com — Mental health support, a therapist directory, and a podcast for Black women.
- **Trauma Research Foundation**
  www.traumaresearchfoundation.org — Trauma-informed programs, research, and healing resources.

## Legal and Advocacy Support

If you're navigating legal concerns or just beginning to understand your rights, here are a few organizations that offer confidential, accessible guidance.

- **WomensLaw.org**
  www.womenslaw.org
  Offers legal information and support for survivors of domestic abuse, including emotional and financial abuse. Features a state-by-state legal guide and an anonymous "Email a Lawyer" service for survivors.
- **National Network to End Domestic Violence (NNEDV)**
  www.nnedv.org
  Provides education, policy advocacy, and a directory of resources—including links to local legal aid and technology safety tips for survivors.
- **Legal Aid Locator (via LawHelp.org)**
  www.lawhelp.org
  Helps people with low and moderate incomes find free legal aid programs in their communities, including help with restraining orders, housing, custody, and financial abuse.

**Remember:** You don't have to do this alone. Support is out there. Healing is possible—and you are worth it.

www.ingramcontent.com/pod-product-compliance
Lightning Source LLC
Chambersburg PA
CBHW020516080526
44583CB00013B/615